Jet Engines

Jet Engines

FUNDAMENTALS OF THEORY, DESIGN AND OPERATION

Klause Hünecke

Motorbooks International
Publishers & Wholesalers ®

This edition first published in 1997 by Motorbooks International Publishers
& Wholesalers, 729 Prospect Avenue, PO Box 1, Osceola, W1 54020 USA

4th impression 2000
Previously published by Airlife Publishing Ltd, Shrewsbury, England.

This is an updated edition of
Flugtriebwerke – Ihre Technik und Funktion by Klaus Huenecke,
first published in Germany in 1987 by Motorbuch Verlag, Stuttgart.
The information in this book is true and complete to the best of our
knowledge. All recommendations are made without any guarantee on the
part of the author or publisher, who also disclaim any liability in connection
with the use of this data or specific details.

We recognize that some words, model names and designations, for example,
mentioned herein are the property of the trademark holder. We use them for
identification purposes only. This is not an official publication.

Motorbooks International books are also available at discounts in bulk
quantity for industrial or sales-promotional use. For details write to Special
Sales Manager at the Publisher's address.

Library of Congress Cataloging-in-Publication Data Available.

ISBN 0-7603-0459-9

Printed and bound in Great Britain by Biddles Ltd, *www.biddles.co.uk*

Preface

This book is concerned with one of the most fascinating machines of modern times – the gas turbine aero-engine. Gas turbine technology is portrayed to provide a concise, well-founded survey of this interesting field of aeronautical engineering, dealing not only with all relevant engine components, but also addressing problems of airframe-engine integration, both for subsonic transports and supersonic fighters.

Material for this book was gathered from distinguished sources throughout the world. A list of engine main data is given in the appendix to make the book also useful as a work of reference.

This book is intended primarily for those who wish to broaden their knowledge about turbine engine technology and the associated problems. The book is likewise suited to engineers in the shops, personnel of airlines and armed forces, and undergraduate students in support of their training.

Klaus Huenecke

Acknowledgements

The material of this book was collected from numerous distinguished sources throughout the world. I would like to express my sincere gratitude to the following institutions (even if names may have changed in the meantime):

Allied Signal Inc, Phoenix, Arizona, USA

The Boeing Company, Seattle, Wash, USA

General Electric Aircraft Engines, Evendale, Ohio, USA

Lockheed Fort Worth, Texas, USA

Lockheed Martin Corp, Bethesda, Maryland, USA

McDonnell Douglas Corp, St Louis, Miss, USA

Northrop Corp, Los Angeles, Calif, USA

Rolls-Royce plc, 65 Buckingham Gate, London, UK

Saab Scania AB, Linköping, Sweden

Turbo-Union Ltd, Bristol, UK

United Technologies Pratt & Whitney, E Hartford, Conn, USA

Volvo Aero Corp, Trollhättan, Sweden

I am particularly grateful to the following persons:
Donald D. Archer (Boeing Flight Test), Walter A. Barron (Grumman), William A. Schoneberger (Northrop), Erwin H. Schuldt and Alexa Oertel (General Electric, Germany), Volker Otto (Garrett), Ernst Simon (Deutsche Lufthansa).

KLAUS HUENECKE

Contents

1. Turbine aircraft propulsion

1.1 History

The idea of utilizing the physical principle of reaction on a large scale by means of rockets is usually attributed to China in the thirteenth century. Not until after the second world war, however, did rocket technology mature to a state which made the idea of space travel a practical possibility, owing largely to a giant step forward during the war itself.

How similar the delay in the development of turbines! Although earliest models of the steam turbine date back to the 17th century, practical application of the turbine engine had to wait until the turn of the 20th century, by competing successfully against the then dominating reciprocating steam engine. Today, the gas turbine engine is the most widespread and most effective method of aircraft propulsion, having almost totally displaced the reciprocating engine which, up to the 1960s, was the common power source in aviation. Appearing in the form of a turbojet, turbofan, turboprop, or turboshaft engine, the gas turbine represents one of the most important technological achievements in aviation, the successful introduction of which made possible a tremendous acceleration of progress in all fields of aviation.

The following historical milestones are worthy of mention as major steps toward turbine engine development, culminating in the use of the gas turbine for aircraft propulsion:

1500 – Leonardo da Vinci portrays a paddle wheel which is driven by ascending hot air to rotate a barbecue spit.

1629 – the Italian engineer Giovanni Branca designs a turbine wheel driven by a steam jet. This appears to be the first known evidence of an axial flow impulse turbine (see Chapter 6).

1687 – the English philosopher and mathematician Sir Isaac Newton formulates three laws of motion which form the basis of modern jet propulsion, according to which:

1. a body remains either at rest, or in motion of constant velocity, unless an external force acts on the body;
2. the sum of forces acting on a body equals the product of the body's mass times acceleration produced by these forces (i.e. force = mass times acceleration);
3. for every force acting on a body, the body exerts a force of equal magnitude and opposite direction along the same line of action as the original force.

As a proof of the third law, an attempt was made to utilize reaction forces to move Newton's steam wagon. Due to excess weight of the boiler structure the attempt failed.

1791 – the Englishman John Barber is granted a patent for a gas-driven turbine engine which utilizes the thermodynamic cycle of the modern gas turbine. Intended as a stationary gas turbine for industrial use, the power plant was to comprise a gas generator with compressor, combustion chamber and a turbine wheel – components that are fundamental to today's engines. The Barber engine was never built, however.

1824 – for the first time in the technical literature the word *turbine* is used. The Frenchman *Burdin* denotes a water wheel designed by him as a turbine.

1883 – the Swedish engineer *Patrik de Laval* runs the first useful steam turbine. The characteristic shape of the nozzle produces super-sonic velocity at nozzle exit (see Chapter 7).

1897 – in England a *Parson* steam turbine to power a ship is tested for the first time. Seven years later the German turbine-driven cruiser *Lubeck* is launched.

1898 – the French *Armangaud* brothers run the first gas turbine engine. Ignition of the gaseous mixture of pressurized air and gas oil is accomplished by heated wires.

1908 – German *Hans Holzwarth* runs a gas turbine with valve-controlled combustion chamber and electrical ignition of the fuel-air mixture.

1913 – the French engineer *Lorin* is granted a patent on a ramjet device. Attempts to build hardware fails due to inadequate materials.

1918 – at General Electric in the United States, *Sanford Moss* develops an exhaust turbo-charger for reciprocating aero-engines. This is the first application of a gas turbine in an aircraft propulsion system.

1930 – *Frank Whittle* of Great Britain applied for his patent 'Improvements relating to the Propulsion of Aircraft and other Vehicles', in which he describes a jet engine with multi-stage axial compressor followed by a centrifugal compressor, annular combustion chamber, single-stage axial turbine, and a nozzle. Based on this patent (British 347,206), the first Whittle engine successfully ran in April, 1937. The engine ran on liquid fuel.

1937 – German engineering scientist *Pabst von Ohain*, employed with the Heinkel aircraft company, runs a turbojet engine producing 250 daN (550 lb) of thrust. Similar to the Whittle design, Ohain's He S-1 engine featured a centrifugal compressor. Engine fuel was gaseous hydrogen to avoid combustion problems.

1939 – a gasoline-burning derivative of Ohain's engine, the He S-3B, developing 500 daN (1100 lb) thrust, at a weight of 360 daN (795 lb), flew in a Heinkel He 178 experimental jet aircraft on the world's first turbojet-powered flight.

1940 – the Junkers Jumo 004 axial-flow turbojet runs at the Junkers engine company in Germany. *Anselm Franz* pioneered development of the axial-flow turbojet, as opposed to the centrifugal-flow designs of the original Whittle and Ohain engines.

1941 – in Great Britain, the Gloster E28/39 experimental jet aircraft flew with Whittle's W1A engine which developed 400 daN (850 lb) of thrust at a weight of 280 daN (623 lb).

1941 – in the US, General Electric was entrusted by the US Army Air Force with developing and producing Whittle-type jet engines which led to the design of the J33 centrifugal-flow compressor engine. Bell was authorized to design the XP-59A experimental aircraft.

1942 – in Germany the Messerschmitt Me-262 twin-engined fighter, powered by the Jumo 004A engine, first flew in July of this year. By March 1945, almost 6000 Jumo 004A jet engines had been built.

1943 – in Great Britain development and production of the Whittle engine is taken over by Rolls-Royce. The Gloster Meteor 1 fighter, powered by two Whittle-type Rolls-Royce Welland engines, enters RAF service in 1944.

These early steps laid the foundation of modern high-thrust engines.

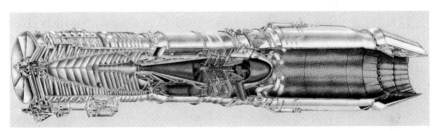

Fig 1-1   The J79 turbojet of General Electric was licence-built in many countries

1.2   Engine classification

According to their task, different types of engine exist. A distinction is made with reference to design characteristics such as number of spools, principle of compression, distribution of airflow within the engine, utilization of the exhaust gas.

Basically, there are four types of turbine engine used in aircraft:

turbojet, turbofan, turboprop, turboshaft.

Turbojet and turbofan engines provide propulsive forces directly by reaction forces generated by the exhaust gas. Turbofan engines, in particular, are classified according to the portion of mass airflow that is bypassed around the basic engine, and are typically denoted as high-bypass or low-bypass-ratio engines.

In a turboprop, the energy of the hot gas is used to drive an additional, but separate turbine, which in turn provides shaft power to drive a propeller. The gas when exhausting from the nozzle, has transmitted most of its energy to the turbines, with a small amount of energy remaining for the generation of thrust.

In a turboshaft engine, all of the usable hot gas energy is extracted and converted into shaft power, by an additional (free) turbine. This type of engine is typically used with helicopters, but is similarly employed in auxiliary power units to provide pneumatic and electric power for aircraft ground operation.

1.2.1 Turbojet engines

The earliest type of a turbo-propulsion engine was the turbojet. Simple by design, but largely superseded through technological progress, a turbojet is made up of the following components (**Fig 1-2**):

> multi-stage compressor
>
> combustor
>
> single or multi-stage turbine

In order to function properly to produce thrust, an *air intake* and an *exhaust system* are required to process the airflow.

The air first enters the intake section which must deliver a smooth and uniform stream of air to the compressor. The compressor is a mechanical device, a fast rotating air 'pump' whose task is to raise the pressure of the air. The resultant energy transfer leads to a rise not only in pressure, but also in temperature and density.

On discharge from the compressor, the pressurized air enters the combustion chamber, where fuel is injected and burned, thus adding

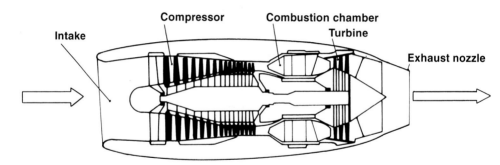

Fig 1-2 Components of a turbojet engine

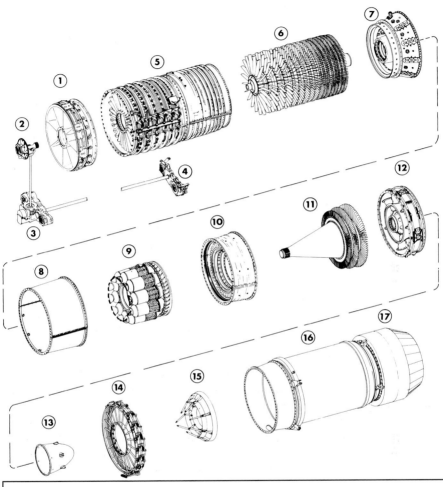

1	Compressor front frame	7	Compressor rear frame	13	Rear cone
2	Bevel gear	8	Combustion casing	14	Reheat fuel manifold
3	Transfer gearbox	9	Combustion assembly		assembly
4	Accessory gearbox	10	Turbine casing	15	Flame holder
5	Compressor casing	11	Turbine rotor	16	Afterburner
6	Rotor	12	Turbine rear frame	17	Exhaust nozzle

Fig 1-3   Components of General Electric J79 turbojet engine

hugely more energy to the airflow. Energy transfer at this section is achieved by a chemical reaction. The combustion process leads to a steep increase in temperature, whereas pressure remains virtually constant. It is here that the airflow is decisively processed to take on the characteristics of a gas useful for gas turbine operation, i.e. to produce mechanical work efficiently.

The first station where energy is absorbed from the gas is in the gas turbine, which gave this class of engines its name. A gas turbine is the complementary part to a compressor, to which it is rigidly linked by a hollow shaft or spool. The task of the turbine is to convert gas energy into mechanical work to drive the compressor, and also some accessories necessary for engine operation.

The energy content of the hot gas is not depleted when the gas discharges from the turbine. In fact, the three components consisting of compressor, combustion chamber and turbine combined have processed the airflow such that a gas is available to do some work. Therefore, these units together are termed a *gas generator*, regardless of engine type.

In a turbojet, as its name implies, a major part of the heat and pressure energy of the gas is still available to be converted into *kinetic energy*. This is the task of the exhaust nozzle which is of characteristic tube-like shape to accomplish energy conversion from heat and pressure to velocity. High exhaust velocity is a prerequisite to the generation of thrust.

Exhaust velocity may be increased further by *afterburning* or *thrust augmentation*, a simple but fuel-exhausting method of adding more heat downstream of the turbine. A famous turbojet of this kind was the General Electric J79 engine which powered the Starfighter and Phantom combat aircraft. Although of dated technology, these aircraft of the fifties and sixties are still flying with some air forces. Layout of the J79 engine nicely illustrates basic component design of turbo-propulsion engines and may conveniently serve to explain modern jet engine technology in subsequent chapters (**Fig 1-3**).

1.2.2   Turboprop engines

The central element of a turbine engine is the *gas generator* which typically comprises *compressor*, *combustion* and *turbine* sections. By adding an inlet and a nozzle, a turbojet results.

If the turbine section of a gas generator is designed so that more energy is abstracted from the hot gas than is necessary to drive the compressor and some auxiliaries, the excess shaft power may be used to drive a propeller (**Fig 1-5**). While the basic layout of a turboprop is similar to a plain turbojet, it differs mainly by:

Fig 1-4   F-104 and F-4 combat aircraft of the sixties, powered by General Electric
J79 turbojet engine

- an additional turbine to drive the propeller,
- a two-spool arrangement of the rotational machinery, and,
- a mechanical reduction gear to convert the high rotational speed
of the turbine to the more moderate speed of the propeller.

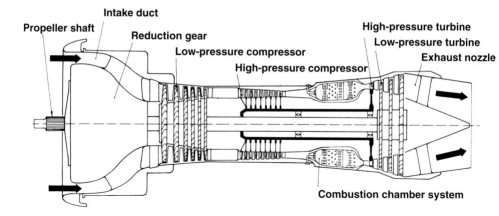

Propeller shaft
Intake duct
Reduction gear
Low-pressure compressor
High-pressure compressor
High-pressure turbine
Low-pressure turbine
Exhaust nozzle
Combustion chamber system

Fig 1-5   Turboprop engine schematic

Whereas a turbojet is designed to accelerate a relative *low* air mass flow to a *high* exhaust velocity, a turboprop conversely is designed to accelerate a *high* mass flow to a *low* velocity. This results in unsurpassed fuel efficiency, although at the expense of flight speed and cabin noise.

Fig 1-6   Lockheed Hercules military transport, powered by four General Motors T56-A-7 turboprops of 4,100 hp each

1.2.3   Turbofan engines

At flight velocities around Mach 0.8 (or 1000 km/h at 11 km altitude, 500 kt at 40,000 ft) turboprop and turbojet engines alike operate at low propulsive efficiency, as this flight speed is too high for the turboprop, but low to the turbojet. The gap is filled by turbofan engines, which exhibit good efficiencies at the high-subsonic cruise velocities important to civil aviation, but are also important to combat aircraft for long-range fuel-efficient cruise well below the high-drag sound barrier (**Fig 1-7**).

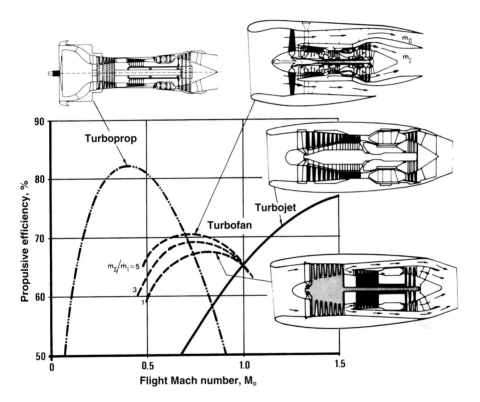

Fig 1-7   Propulsive efficiency characteristics of turboprop, turbofan and turbojet engines

The turbofan has emerged as the most common type of a gas turbine engine for aircraft propulsion. Similar to that of the turboprop, the turbine section is designed to absorb more energy from the hot gas than would be necessary to drive the compressor alone. The excess shaft power is used to drive a *fan*, a low-pressure compressor of larger diameter arranged upstream of the main compressor. Part of the air entering

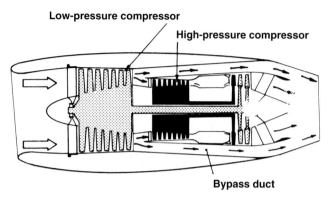

Fig 1-8   Turbofan engine schematic

the engine intake, after being processed in the fan section, bypasses the inner or *core* engine and expands in a separate nozzle to provide 'cold' thrust; some types mix the cold flow with the hot exhaust gas from the core engine to increase propulsive efficiency (as in the V.2500 engine) (**Fig 1-8**).

The amount of air that is bypassed in relation to the air that passes through the core engine is termed the *bypass-ratio*. A distinction is made between low and high bypass-ratio engines, the former being employed with supersonic combat aircraft and the latter with high-subsonic military and commercial transport aircraft.

1.2.3.1 Low bypass-ratio turbofan engines
In terms of performance, the bottom line today is fuel efficiency. Through bypassing, modern engines use less fuel than earlier engines of comparable thrust, but without this technology.

A bypass ratio in the range of 0.2:1 to 1:1 is classified a *low bypass-ratio*. This means the amount of airflow bypassed around the core engine is of the order of 20 to 100 per cent of that which passes through the core, or if referenced to the total ingested air mass, 5 to 50 per cent of the intake airflow is bypassed around the core.

Bypass-ratios of 1 were utilized with early turbofan equipped airliners of the sixties such as the Boeing 727, which had three Pratt & Whitney JT8D turbofans of bypass-ratio one. The relatively high exhaust velocities of these engines generate noise levels which nowadays are intolerable for civil application, thus precluding the low bypass-ratio turbofan from further use with commercial airliners. However, this class of engines is widely used with modern combat aircraft, and due to its fuel economy at high-subsonic flight speeds, the low bypass-ratio turbofan provides the fighter with increased radius-of-action.

Fig 1-9   Lockheed C-141 powered by four Pratt & Whitney TF33-P-7A turbofans

Fig 1-10   Pratt & Whitney TF33-P-7A turbofan (thrust 9,500 daN, 16-stage compressor, 4-stage turbine, compressor pressure ratio 14:1)

Fig 1-11   General Dynamics F-111 combat aircraft powered by two Pratt & Whitney TF30-P-7 turbofans

Fig 1-12   Pratt & Whitney TF30-P-7 turbofan (thrust 9,200 daN, 16-stage compressor, 4-stage turbine, compressor pressure ratio 17.5:1)

1.2.3.2 High bypass-ratio turbofans

The economy of transport aircraft was greatly improved with the advent of the high bypass-ratio turbofan. First introduced with the Lockheed C5-A military transport, this technology was quickly adopted for civil use.

Engines of bypass-ratio 5:1 and more are classified as *high bypass-ratio engines*. These found their first civilian use in the late sixties with high-capacity wide-body airliners such as the Boeing 747, Lockheed L-1011 TriStar and McDonnell Douglas DC-10.

A typical feature of this type of engine is the large single-stage fan operating upstream of the basic or core engine from which it is directly driven (**Fig 1-13**)). The core engine primarily acts as a *gas generator* which provides a high-energy gas flow to drive the fan turbine, additionally to the turbine of the core engine. The major advantage of the high bypass-ratio turbofan is its high thrust level, especially at take-off, which results largely from accelerating a large air mass bypassing the core, whereas thrust from the core engine is only about 15% of total engine thrust. In addition, the high bypass-ratio turbofan burns fuel very economically by comparison with the low BPR engine, or even the pure jet at the same flight speed; but not, however, as economically as the turboprop. Also, noise emission from the high BPR turbofan is relatively low due to the low exhaust velocities of the propulsive jet.

High bypass-ratio engines were conceived in the US in the early sixties, starting from research programs aimed at developing both an advanced-technology gas generator and a high bypass-ratio fan. In 1961 the two largest US manufacturers of aircraft engines, General

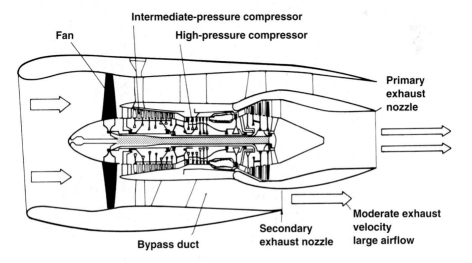

Fig 1-13   Rolls-Royce RB.211 high bypass-ratio turbofan, schematic

Electric and Pratt & Whitney, started development of advanced core engines: Pratt & Whitney with a lightweight gas generator and General Electric with the GE1 'building block' which was to provide the basis for a whole family of new power units. P&W also started design of its 'Advanced Technology Engine' (ATE) which in 1964 led to the testing of the STF200 experimental turbofan. This delivered 140 kN/31,000 lb of thrust from a 2:1 bypass-ratio engine (in contrast to today's engines which deliver up to 340 kN/76,000 lb). Other US companies contributed with engineering studies sponsored by the US Air Force that in the case of Lycoming led to the testing of a 6:1 bypass-ratio fan engine. The connection between these various developments was a USAF requirement to power the giant C-5A Galaxy transport aircraft. The sheer size of this aircraft stipulated typical propulsion characteristics of high thrust on take-off and low specific fuel consumption at cruising flight, both of which implied the use of a high bypass-ratio and a high turbine inlet temperature.

Fig 1-14 Lockheed C-5A military transport powered by four General Electric
TF39 high bypass-ratio turbofans

Both companies, GE and P&W, during the C-5A competition were requested by the USAF to increase bypass-ratios in their proposals. Subsequently P&W entered its 180 kN (40,000 lb) thrust, 3.4:1 bypass-ratio JTF14E derivative of the STF200; and GE used a 2/3 scale GE1/6 engine with 8:1 bypass-ratio fan featuring one and one half stages. As a result of the competition, General Electric in August 1965 was awarded the largest-ever US military engine contract, worth $459 million, to develop and supply the 183 kN (41,000 lb) thrust, 8:1 bypass-ratio TF39 engine for the C-5A.

Fig 1-15 General Electric TF39 high bypass-ratio turbofan (thrust 18,600 daN, bypass-ratio 8:1, compressor pressure ratio 25.7:1)

Pratt & Whitney, after losing in the C5 competition, continued development of its JTF14E in a company-funded test program which provided the technical basis for a big new civil turbofan, the JT9D engine, of 183 kN (41,000 lb) thrust and 5:1 bypass-ratio (**Fig 1-16**). Discussions about possible commercial applications were made with Boeing and McDonnell Douglas, also losing contestants in the C-5A competition. In the event, the JT9D was selected to power the Boeing 747, with Pan American placing its historic order in April 1966. Although GE had attempted to enter the civil big-fan market with its CTF39 (a civil version of the TF39 for the C-5A) the 8:1 bypass-ratio of the TF39 proved ill-matched to commercial transports.

In Europe, Rolls-Royce emerged as the sole supplier of high bypass-ratio turbofans. In 1961 the British company began design studies for a large new two-shaft civil turbofan, the RB178, with financial support from the Ministry of Aviation. The engine with a bypass ratio 2.3:1 ran in July, 1966, delivering 125 kN (28,000 lb) of thrust, but was tested for a total time of only five hours. In order to be technically competitive, Rolls-Royce had decided that a three-shaft engine of much higher rating and bypass-ratio was necessary.

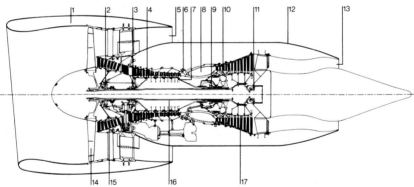

1 Fan casing
2 Bearing No. 1
3 Bearing No. 2
4 High-pressure compressor, 11 stages
5 Fan exhaust nozzle
6 20 fuel injection nozzles
7 Hp-rotor (N$_2$), max 7,580rpm
8 Annular combustion chamber
9 Bearing No.3

10 2-stage high-pressure turbine
11 Bearing No. 4
12 Core engine casing
13 Core exhaust nozzle
14 Fan rotor
15 3-stage low-pressure compressor
16 Lp-rotor (N$_1$), max 3,350rpm
17 Low-pressure turbine, 4 stages

Fig 1-16 Pratt & Whitney JT9D-7 high bypass-ratio turbofan powering first generation of Boeing 747 wide body transports (thrust 20,600 daN, bypass-ratio 5:1, compressor pressure ratio 24:1, mass flow rate 680 kg/s)

Fig 1-17   Boeing 747 powered by four Pratt & Whitney JT9D-7 high bypass-ratio turbofans

In the course of the development two variants came out: the RB207 of 5:1 bypass-ratio and 211 kN (47,500 lb) thrust for the European Airbus as well as for the Douglas and Lockheed twin-engined projects, and the RB211 of 5:1 bypass ratio and 147 kN (33,000 lb) thrust for the American trijet projects that were later to become the DC-10 and L-1011 airliners. Initial US twinjet studies did not mature.

For the Airbus projects, both GE and P&W prepared suitable engine proposals: P&W a scaled-down derivative of its JT9D – the JT18D of 5:1 bypass-ratio and 156 kN (35,000 lb) thrust; GE the CF6/34 of 6:1 bypass-ratio and 151 kN (34,000 lb) thrust, derived from the TF39, from which the core engine was retained, but with a smaller fan and a modified low-pressure turbine to drive the fan.

The outcome of these various developments was that General Electric was chosen in April 1968 to power the DC-10 trijet with its CF6-6 of 178 kN (40,000 lb), and Rolls-Royce in March 1968 to power the L-1011 TriStar with its RB211-22 of 187 kN (42,000 lb). The British Government had earlier withdrawn from the Airbus A300 project, and P&W withdrew its offer of the JT18D.

GE's decision in 1969 to go ahead with its CF6-50 series delivering between 218 kN (49,000 lb) and 240 kN (54,000 lb) thrust not only contributed to the sales potential of the DC-10, but also gained access to the B-747 and was instrumental in launching the European Airbus A300.

While development of the 'big' fans was pursued with great effort by

Fig 1-18   Lockheed TriStar powered by three Rolls-Royce RB211 high bypass-ratio turbofans

Fig 1-19   McDonnell Douglas DC-10 powered by three General Electric CF6 high bypass-ratio turbofans

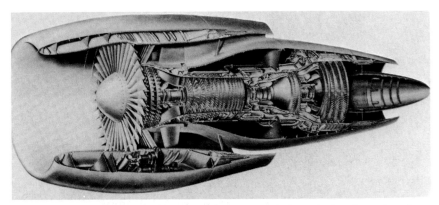

Fig 1-20   General Electric CF6-50A high bypass-ratio turbofan, featuring three booster stages downstream of fan (thrust 22,200 daN, bypass ratio 5:1, compressor pressure ratio 28.4:1)

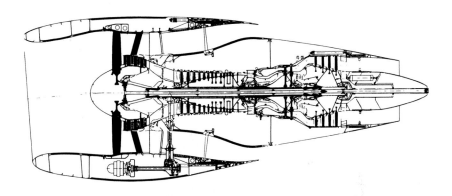

the three large engine manufacturers, progress of the smaller bypass-ratio turbofans was less vigorous.

In 1971 *General Electric* teamed with French engine manufacturer *Snecma* to develop an engine of 'ten ton' thrust. The first example of this, the CFM56, ran in June 1974, well ahead of a demand. First application came with the McDonnell Douglas DC-8 airliners that were to be re-engined with the CFM56-2 of 107 kN (24,000 lb) thrust, making the aircraft much more fuel-efficient than it had been with the original low bypass-ratio engines. Subsequently, the '-2' engines were also used to re-engine the KC-135 tanker fleet of the USAF. In 1985 the CFM56-3 variant of 89 kN (20,000 lb) thrust entered service with

Fig 1-21   Sikorsky CH-53G helicopter powered by two General Electric T64 turboshaft engines

the Boeing 737-300 medium range airliner giving new life to the dated 737 design. The greatest success of the ten ton CFM56 came, however, when it enabled Airbus Industrie to launch its A320, a 150-seat medium-range airliner of advanced technology, which entered service in 1988.

Competing with the CFM56 turbofan for the Airbus was the IAE V.2500 turbofan of 117 kN (25,000 lb) thrust, manufactured by the International Aero Engines (IAE) consortium in which Rolls-Royce teamed with Pratt & Whitney and German, Italian and Japanese aero-engine makers. The V.2500 engine, an all-new design, benefited from the newest technology that gave it better fuel consumption figures than the earlier CFM56. The engine entered service, also on the A320, in 1988.

What made the high bypass-ratio turbofan such a success was the increasing public awareness of atmospheric pollution, in particular aircraft noise. Adding to this success was that in 1985 the majority of US airports were banning the use of aircraft with some of the original low bypass-ratio turbofans – hence the reason for re-engining the DC-8 with low-noise engines.

The relatively low exhaust velocity of the bypassed airflow causes much less noise in the atmosphere, while at the same time unsurpassed thrust levels exist due to the large air mass that is accelerated in the

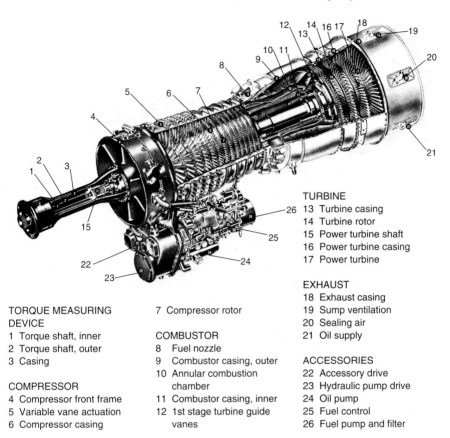

TURBINE
13 Turbine casing
14 Turbine rotor
15 Power turbine shaft
16 Power turbine casing
17 Power turbine

EXHAUST
18 Exhaust casing
19 Sump ventilation
20 Sealing air
21 Oil supply

TORQUE MEASURING
DEVICE
1 Torque shaft, inner
2 Torque shaft, outer
3 Casing

COMPRESSOR
4 Compressor front frame
5 Variable vane actuation
6 Compressor casing

7 Compressor rotor

COMBUSTOR
8 Fuel nozzle
9 Combustor casing, outer
10 Annular combustion
    chamber
11 Combustor casing, inner
12 1st stage turbine guide
    vanes

ACCESSORIES
22 Accessory drive
23 Hydraulic pump drive
24 Oil pump
25 Fuel control
26 Fuel pump and filter

Fig 1-22   General Electric T64 turboshaft engine delivering 4000 hp

bypass duct. Excess power of the high bypass-ratio engine at low flight velocity is ample for aircraft even to take off at reduced thrust, which not only reduces noise still further, but also contributes to engine life.

1.2.4 Turboshaft engines

A turboshaft is similar to a turboprop engine, differing primarily in the task of the second turbine. Instead of driving a propeller, the turbine-driven shaft is connected to a transmission system which drives helicopter rotor blades (**Fig 1-22**).

The compressor of a turboshaft engine first raises the pressure of the incoming air which is then guided into the combustion chamber. After being mixed with vaporized fuel and burned, the hot gas expands completely through two separate turbines. The first of these drives the compressor, the second delivers 'shaft horsepower' to drive the

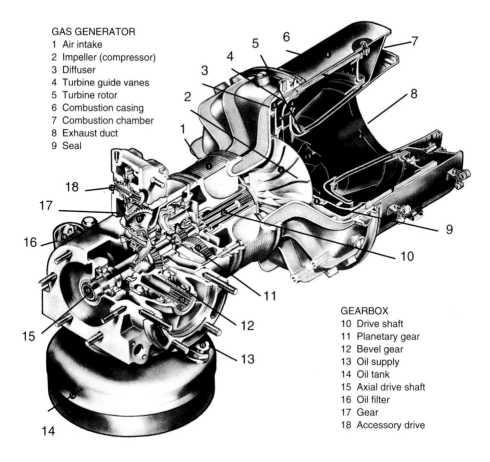

GAS GENERATOR
1 Air intake
2 Impeller (compressor)
3 Diffuser
4 Turbine guide vanes
5 Turbine rotor
6 Combustion casing
7 Combustion chamber
8 Exhaust duct
9 Seal

GEARBOX
10 Drive shaft
11 Planetary gear
12 Bevel gear
13 Oil supply
14 Oil tank
15 Axial drive shaft
16 Oil filter
17 Gear
18 Accessory drive

Fig 1-23   Airborne turboshaft engine Solar T-62T-27 to generate electricity and airflow for engine starting

helicopter rotor via a transmission gear. The gas is finally released through an exhaust duct without producing any thrust.

A special class of turboshaft engine is used for *auxiliary power units* (APU) to provide air conditioning, main engine starting, and to serve as a backup electrical power source in the air and on the ground, rendering aircraft independent from ground support equipment (**Fig 1-23**). In the non-aviation field, turboshaft engines are used as industrial gas turbines to drive, for example, stationary power generators, ships and army tanks.

Turboshaft engines employed in aircraft are of a small size.

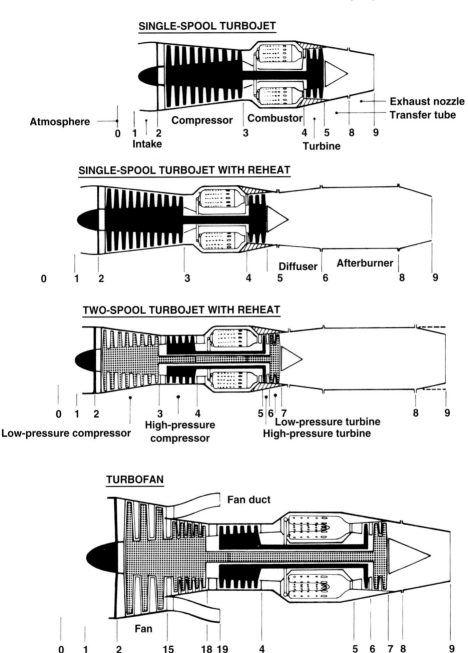

Fig 1-24   Engine station designation

1.3   Engine station designation

For the purpose of estimating engine performance, the engine is regarded as an orderly assembly of components which conform to the definition of stations used in (one-dimensional) calculation of aerothermodynamic performance (**Fig 1-24**). The implication is to provide a convenient basis for component performance description and overall performance estimation.

Designation starts at station 0 denoting undisturbed flow well ahead of the inlet, and ends at station 9 denoting exhaust flow condition of the core engine at nozzle exit. Bypass duct stations are designated like-wise, but by two-digit numbers, the first digit always being a 1, starting at number 12 to denote inlet fan tip section and ending at number 19 to denote bypass exhaust nozzle discharge (**Table 1-1**). The system is generally agreed by industry and related research organizations.

	Core engine		Bypass duct	
	Station No.	Station designation	Station No.	Station designation
	0	undisturbed flow upstream of inlet ("upstream infinity")		identical with core
	1	inlet throat		identical with core
Compressor section	2	low-pressure (l-p) compressor inlet/ fan inlet hub section	12	fan inlet (tip section)
	21	l-p compressor discharge		
	22	intermediate-pressure (i-p) compressor inlet		
	23	i-p compressor discharge		
	24	high-pressure (h-p) compressor inlet		
	3	h-p compressor discharge	13	fan discharge (tip section)
Turbine section	4	h-p turbine inlet		
	41	h-p turbine discharge		
	42	i-p turbine inlet		
	43	i-p turbine discharge		
	44	l-p turbine inlet		
	5	l-p turbine discharge		
Exhaust section	6	afterburner (augmentor) inlet	16	Bypass duct mixer inlet
	7	exhaust nozzle inlet	17	Bypass duct exhaust nozzle interface
	8	exhaust nozzle throat	18	Bypass duct exhaust nozzle throat
	9	exhaust nozzle discharge	19	Bypass duct exhaust nozzle discharge

Table 1-1

2. Jet engine fundamentals

In order to understand how the aircraft gas turbine engine operates, one should be familiar with some of the essential physics laws that govern the field of turbopropulsion. Although a gas turbine appears to operate in an essentially simple manner, a closer examination reveals it to be a highly complex machine, with many interdependent and diverse interactions. A brief presentation of elementary principles is therefore in order without, however, involving complex maths.

Our short course will begin with gas characteristics, deal with general thrust considerations, and will explain some of the most frequently used engine performance parameters.

2.1   Gas characteristics

Aviation turbine engines use as their working substance a hot gas which is compounded of air and the gaseous products of burned fuel. Combustion products result from a chemical reaction between oxygen contained in the ambient airflow ingested through the air intake, and fuel which the aircraft carries on board. The mass ratio is that about 2 per cent of fuel and 98 per cent of air contribute to the gas which propels an aircraft at cruise conditions.

Air which the engine uses as a working fluid, is itself a mixture of gases, mainly nitrogen and oxygen, in the proportion of approximately 20 per cent oxygen and 80 per cent nitrogen. Small and varying quantities of other gases such as carbon dioxide, helium, and neon have no practical effect on gas turbine operation. Of the two main gases, oxygen is necessary for combusting the fuel to generate heat, whereas nitrogen, being an inert gas, generates oxidation products which, although of small amount, have become of major concern in atmospheric pollution.

A gas, when viewed microscopically, generally consists of molecules which move freely (and invisibly) at high speed. As molecules are considered to be particles, laws of mechanics may be applied to them.

Particle motion depends on the temperature of the gas. Conversely, temperature is a measure of the kinetic energy of the molecules. The higher the temperature, the faster molecules move. If heat is added to a gas, the gas will expand because the molecules move faster. This is what happens in a combustion chamber. If expansion of the gas is impeded, pressure will rise.

In addition, molecules are considered to be perfectly elastic particles which, due to their ceaseless motion, randomly collide with each other or with solid walls containing the gas. When colliding with walls, molecules exert a pressure upon them.

These are the underlying principles that make up a special branch in physics known as *kinetic gas theory*. We will not go into greater detail here as this is the task of relevant textbooks. But we would emphasize the point that temperature, pressure, and density, so vital for jet engine functioning, originate from molecular motion.

In a turbine engine, as in many other mechanical applications, use is made of a unique property of gas molecules, namely that energy in terms of temperature and pressure may easily be stored in, and retrieved from them. The energy level a gas has attained at a given station of the engine then shows up by its physical state variables such as pressure, temperature and density.

We will briefly consider these three main variables of state for air:

The *pressure* of a gas is defined as force per unit area acting on a surface:

$$\text{pressure} = \frac{\text{force}}{\text{unit area}}$$

In the International System of Units (SI units) force is measured in Newtons, symbolized N ($1N = 1$ mkg/s^2), and unit area in square meters, m^2. Thus the dimension of a pressure is N/m^2, daN/m^2, or daN/cm^2, the choice being made primarily to avoid numeric values from getting too large.

If the Anglo-American system of units is preferred, weight force is measured in pounds, symbolized lb (from Latin *libra* = balance), and unit area in square feet, sq ft. Thus, the dimension of a pressure is lb/sq ft, or lb/sq in (for conversion *cf* Chapter 2.6).

Some of the components of a gas turbine engine are categorized according to pressure levels to indicate the severity of the operating environment, for example high-pressure compressor, low-pressure turbine, etc. Typical pressures in a jet engine are constantly measured to monitor engine condition, and are indicated on appropriate instruments in the cockpit.

Temperature, the second variable of state, is a measure of the kinetic energy of the molecules and indicates 'hotness' of a body. Scientifically, temperature is a property determining the rate at which heat will be transferred to or from molecules.

Temperature may be measured both in degrees Kelvin and Centigrade, if SI and metric units are used, or in degrees Rankine and Fahrenheit, if Imperial units are preferred. Degrees Kelvin and

Rankine are *absolute* temperatures, i.e. at zero degrees Kelvin or Rankine molecular motion theoretically ceases, whereas degrees Centigrade and Fahrenheit are related to defined reference values. For example, the freezing point of water is arbitrarily defined as zero degrees Centigrade. In jet engine design, absolute temperatures are preferred as they simplify calculations. Engine temperatures in the cockpit, however, are indicated in degrees Centigrade, for example exhaust gas temperature (EGT).

The third state variable of a substance is *density*, symbolized ρ (Greek rho), defined as mass per unit volume. In SI units, the dimension of density is kilograms per cubic metre, kg/m^3; in Anglo-American units slugs per cubic foot, or lb/cu ft. The inverse of the density ρ (rho) is *specific volume* $v = 1/\rho$, with dimension m^3/kg in SI units.

Density indicates the number of molecules contained in a unit volume. For a gas, in particular, this number varies with temperature and pressure. The variation in density is one of the most important properties of a gas, in which it differs from liquids whose number of molecules remains broadly constant whatever the temperature and pressure.

Engine thrust depends directly on the density of air: the higher the density, the more thrust there is available. If airports are at some considerable elevation, and especially at hot ambient temperatures, engine thrust performance can become critical. One such airport where 'hot and high' conditions have to be taken into account by aircraft manufacturers is Denver, Colorado, in the US.

The interrelation between the three state variables density, temperature and pressure is expressed by the equation of an ideal gas:

$$p/\rho = RT$$

R is termed the gas constant (definition in relevant textbooks).

2.2   Engine cycle

The aviation gas turbine is categorized as a *heat engine*. It uses gas as its working fluid and produces (mechanical) shaft power and thrust. Generating thrust, in particular, is possible only if the exhaust velocity of the gas is higher than the velocity at which air enters the engine. In order to accelerate the gas, energy must be added to the airflow within the engine which can then be converted into kinetic energy.

In a gas turbine engine, the increase of energy is accomplished in two consecutive steps, and by two different, though adjacent, engine components. First, pressure of the airflow is raised by the action of mechanical shaft power. This is done in the *compressor* section. After

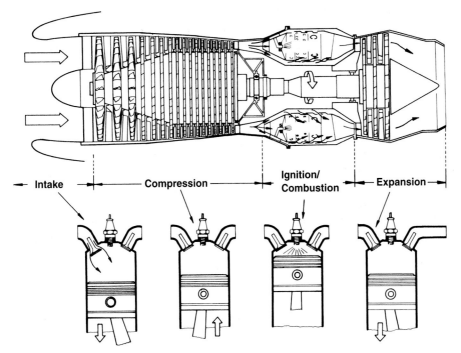

| Intake | Compression | Ignition/ Combustion | Expansion |

Fig 2-1   Comparison of working cycles for turbojet engine and 4-stroke piston engine

its discharge from the compressor, the pressurized air is heated in the *combustion chamber*, where the temperature of the gas is steeply raised.

The gas is now sufficiently processed to provide physical work, i.e. the energetic state of the molecules is high enough for energy to be effectively retrieved from them.

The first station within the engine where work is extracted from the hot gas is the *turbine*. As the gas expands and accelerates, it rotates the turbine. After discharging from the turbine, the gas is further accelerated in the *exhaust nozzle*, where all remaining usable heat energy is converted into kinetic energy.

At nozzle discharge, the gas is ejected to the atmosphere at high velocity, where it will gradually dissipate to the conditions of the surrounding atmosphere. The series of changes of the state variables, by which the gas finally reverts to its original condition, is termed an *engine cycle*.

To explain the operating principle of a gas turbine by means of a technical application with which we are familiar, a comparison is frequently made with the four-stroke reciprocating engine (**Fig 2-1**).

In both cases, the gas is processed in four steps (or strokes in the case of the piston engine) known as induction, compression, combustion and expansion. The fundamental difference, however is, that in the reciprocating engine all four strokes take place in the cylinder concerned, whereas in a turbine engine separate components are assigned to each processing step, making the engine cycle *continuous*, as opposed to *intermittent* in the piston engine.

The induction stroke in the reciprocating engine is comparable to the air intake step of the turbine engine, and the compression stroke compares to the rotating compressor action in the turbine. The combustion process is rather different, however. In the reciprocating engine, combustion occurs at *constant volume*, with pressure peaking at the upper position of the piston, whereas in a turbine engine combustion occurs at *constant pressure*. This allows large masses of air to be processed with lightweight combustion chamber components, and it further permits low-octane fuels to be used.

Finally, when comparing the expansion stroke of the piston engine with that of the jet engine, the analogy becomes questionable, because the exhaust products of the piston engine are not usable, whereas in a jet engine the essential propulsive forces result from the exhaust gas. In this respect, the piston engine more closely resembles a turboshaft engine.

The absence of reciprocating parts in a turbine engine is the greatest advantage over the piston engine, as more energy can be released for a given engine size. Extracting comparable power levels from a piston engine would make it very large, extremely heavy and practically impossible to manufacture, and certainly would preclude its use in the weight-conscious field of aviation.

The change of the variables of state to which the gas is subjected when passing through the engine, can be illustrated in a *pressure–volume diagram*, in which the area bounded by the four curves is a measure of the heat added. This heat can be released for work, either to produce mechanical shaft power or propulsive thrust (**Fig 2-2**).

A more common graphical representation, however, is the *enthalpy–entropy diagram*, where the different forms of energy (mechanical, kinetic, heat) appear as distances that make component assessment much easier (**Fig 2-2**). *Enthalpy* is a thermodynamic quantity denoting total energy of the gas as it undergoes changes from one state to another (symbolized H or h, with dimension J/kg in SI units, ft lb/lbm in Imperial units). *Entropy*, a thermodynamic quantity, denotes a theoretical measure of energy which cannot be transformed into mechanical work, thus being a measure of the quality, or usability of heat. More specifically, to convert heat into mechanical work requires a differential in temperature to exist. The higher the tempera-

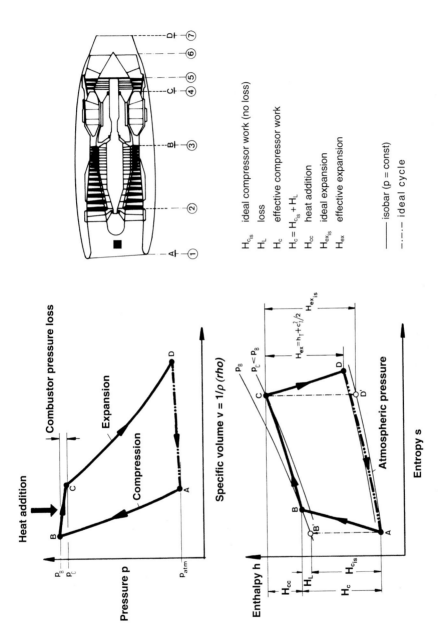

Fig 2-2 Gas turbine working cycle in pressure-volume and enthalpy-entropy diagram

ture of a gas, the better can its heat content be used and converted into work. Entropy is, too, a variable of state of a gas, but it does not lend itself as easily to perceptual description as do temperature and pressure, for example.

Now, let us revert to the diagrams representing a (simplified) jet engine cycle. In both diagrams, point A indicates atmospheric condition of the air as it enters the engine. The compression process is along line A–B, with point B denoting condition of the airflow when discharging from the compressor. While the gas is progressively compressed, its volume progressively decreases. Also, due to friction of the gas along the gas path, more mechanical work has to be expended to achieve the required pressure (point B) than would have been necessary if the flow were ideal (point B^1).

Heat is added to the compressed air along line B–C. Maximum efficiency of the combustion process requires pressure in the combustion chamber to be kept constant. Due to fluid dynamic friction and turbulence, a small drop in pressure always occurs within the combustion chamber (point C).

Expansion in the turbine and exhaust nozzle is along line C–D. The available energy, too, is less than would be possible in frictionless flow (point D^1). Also, the exhausting jet rarely expands to atmospheric pressure, another source of insufficient use of the gas energy.

Apart from readily showing how flow conditions change within the engine, it also becomes apparent from these diagrams that the engine designer is confronted with numerous sources of thermodynamic and fluid losses originating at the different engine components.

2.3   Thrust

Propulsion of a jet aircraft is accomplished by the principle of reaction: a gas jet exhausting at high velocity from a nozzle generates a force in the opposite direction that is termed *thrust* (**Fig 2-3**).

The amount of thrust depends on the mass of the airflow passing through the engine, and the exhaust velocity. The product of mass m and velocity v is termed *momentum*, a name given to this quantity by Descartes (1644):

momentum I = mass m × velocity v
Dimension is mkg/s^2 in SI units.

Whenever there is a variation in momentum (an event that will take some time), a force will be generated. This is the underlying principle which forms the basis of jet propulsion. It has become known as the *theorem of momentum*, but is commonly denoted as the thrust equa-

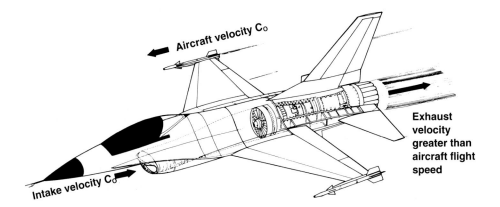

Fig 2-3   Thrust produced by a jet exiting at high velocity from a nozzle

tion. Basically, a jet engine represents a machine whose purpose is to increase (i.e. to change) the momentum mv of the airstream passing through it.

Application in practice is straightforward and allows engine thrust to be calculated fairly easily, the primary advantage being that knowledge of conditions within the engine is not required. Only the conditions at the boundaries of the jet engine matter.

Calculating engine thrust follows a stepwise procedure. The first step is to define a meaningful control volume, as required by the theorem of momentum (**Fig 2-4**).

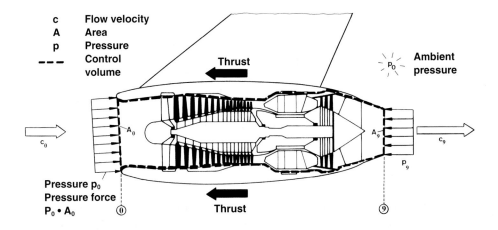

Fig 2-4   Explaining the momentum theorem

In the second step, all known and unknown forces acting at the boundaries of the control volume must be listed and their sum formed. Note that a distinction has to be made between *solid boundaries* through which airflow cannot pass, and *gaseous boundaries* which will let airflow (and thus momentum) pass through.

In the example given, engine stations 0 and 9 represent open boundaries through which the airflow is allowed to pass. The only forces that can act on them are pressure forces. The other boundaries are solid walls that make up the engine casing, on which both pressure and friction forces act. These forces are considered as unknown, they constitute engine thrust which is the aim of our calculation procedure.

When dealing with forces, it should be noted, that forces (like velocities) are *vector* quantities which not only have a magnitude, but also a direction. As thrust is considered to act into the direction of flight, and the flow approaches from left, the thrust vector also points to the left, bearing a negative sign ($-T$). With this assumption, all forces acting on the engine may be formed as follows:

pressure force, plane 0: $+p_0 A_0$ (pressure force = pressure × area)
pressure forces, plane 9: (in flight direction, i.e. negative):
        a) acting at area less exit of exhaust nozzle: $-p_0(A_0-A_9)$
        b) acting at exit area of exhaust nozzle: $-p_9 A_9$
thrust force (acting in flight direction): $-T$

Summing all forces in horizontal direction:
Sum = $+ p_0 A_0 - p_0(A_0-A_9) - p_9 A_9 -T = A_9 (p_0-p_9) -T$

The third step is to determine the timewise variation of the momentum, i.e. momentum divided by time, which is equal to the sum of all forces:

$$\frac{momentum}{time} = \frac{mass \times velocity}{time}$$

The variation in momentum emerges as a product of two quantities: 'mass divided by time' and 'velocity'. The quantity 'mass divided by time' is the airflow passing through the engine in a given time, and is termed *mass flow rate*, with dimension kg/s in SI units, lb/s in British units. Hence, the timewise variation of the momentum is the product of mass flow rate and a velocity. In the case of a jet engine, this velocity is the exhaust velocity.

The above deduction is, strictly, valid only for the engine at rest, i.e. before taking off at zero aircraft velocity. In flight at velocity v_0, the airflow approaching the engine already carries with it an 'intake momentum' $\dot{m} * v_0$, which has to be deducted when calculating thrust.

Considering all the effects stated, the thrust equation assumes the following (simplified) form:

$$-T = \dot{m}(c_9 - v_0) + A_9\,(p_9-p_0)$$

$\dot{m}$	mass rate of flow, kg/s
c_9	jet exhaust velocity, m/s
v_0	intake velocity, m/s
p	static pressure, N/m^2
A	area, m^2
subscript 0	intake station
subscript 9	exhaust station

Example

a) Assumptions:

$p_9 = p_0$	the exhausting jet expands to ambient pressure
$v_0 = 0$	aircraft at rest
$\dot{m} = 50$ kg/s	mass flow rate
$c_9 = 600$ m/s	exhaust velocity

Result:
$$-T = 50 \times 600 = 30{,}000 \text{ m } \frac{\text{kg}}{\text{s}^2} = 30 \text{ kN}$$

The dimension of thrust is frequently given in kilo-Newton, kN, or Deka-Newton, daN when using SI units.

m = 110lb$_m$ mass flow rate

V_{exit} = 1970 ft/sec

$$T = \frac{m}{g_c}\,(V_{exit} - V_{inlet})$$

$$= \frac{110\text{lb}_m/\text{sec}* (1970\text{ft/sec} - 0\text{ft/sec})}{32.2\text{lb}_m \text{ ft/lb sec}^2} = 6735 \text{ lb}$$

2.4   Basic laws in fluid dynamics

As many flow phenomena follow a regular pattern, their behaviour is entirely predictable. This property is also made use of in fluid dynamics, which is a special branch of physics.

2.4.1   Types of flow

Flow passing through a duct may be either steady or unsteady. The flow is considered *steady*, if fluid parameters like velocity, pressure, temperature remain constant at any arbitrary cross section of the duct. Their values may vary, however, from one section to another along the flow path. The overall streamline pattern essentially remains unchanged with time. In a jet engine at cruising flight conditions, for example, flow parameters are constant everywhere.

At compressor discharge there is high pressure of the airflow, low velocity, and elevated temperature due to the compression action. Similarly, flow parameters are also constant at turbine discharge, though at a different level, characterized by much higher temperature and velocity, but lower pressure.

A flow is considered *unsteady*, if typical flow parameters at any one cross section change with time. Unsteady phenomena in a turbojet engine occur during acceleration and deceleration when adjusting thrust. Flow in a reciprocating engine is unsteady throughout.

2.4.2   Streamline and streamtube

Fluid motion, when viewed microscopically, consists of an inconceivably large number of molecular particles in motion. If we pursue the path of the particles through a tube (which may be an exhaust nozzle), these particles are seen to flow along streamlines. A characteristic of a streamline is its tangent which at any station points into the direction of the velocity vector. Streamtubes envelope a number of streamlines passing through a closed curve transverse to the flow. A streamline may be thought of as a tube having gaseous walls within which the fluid flows. A streamtube is made up of ever changing particles. At steady flow conditions, a streamtube behaves like a real tube with solid walls.

In general, streamlines move closer to each other as the area of the streamtube decreases, indicating accelerating flow (**Fig 2-5**). This is what happens in a convergent nozzle. Conversely, as cross sectional

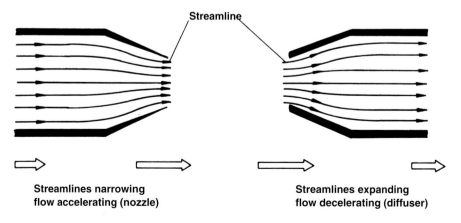

Streamlines narrowing
flow accelerating (nozzle)

Streamlines expanding
flow decelerating (diffuser)

Fig 2-5   Effect of narrowing and expanding streamlines

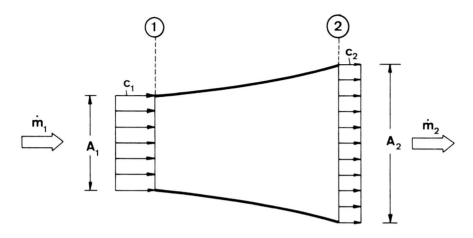

Fig 2-6   Explaining conservation of mass

area increases in streamwise direction, streamlines move farther apart
from each other indicating decelerating flow. This is what happens in
a diffuser, such as a conventional (subsonic) air intake.

2.4.3 Conservation of matter

One of the fundamental concepts of physics is that matter cannot
vanish. This is of great significance in predicting fluid flow behaviour.

For steady-state fluid motion, the continuity of matter may be
expressed by using the concept of streamlines. The continuity of matter
simply states that the same amount of fluid must flow through every
cross section of a streamtube; fluid cannot vanish within that tube. If
the shape of the tube is known, as for example in an exhaust nozzle
where the whole nozzle may be regarded as a streamtube, flow characteristics may be calculated very simply.

This can be demonstrated by first assuming that fluid velocity V_1 is
evenly distributed across the inlet streamtube area A_1 (**Fig 2-6**). A fluid
flow of volume Q per second entering a streamtube of cross sectional
area A_1 results in a volumetric flow rate of:

Flow Rate = $V_1 A_1$

Mass flow rate $\dot{m}$ follows by multiplying volume flow rate with
density ρ (Greek rho):

$\dot{m}_1 = \rho_1 V_1 A_1$

In the same manner, airflow leaving the tube is calculated:

$\dot{m}_2 = \rho_2 V_2 A_2$

As mass flow rates both are equal according to the mass conservation law, exhaust velocity V_2 immediately follows:

$$V_2 = \frac{\rho_1}{\rho_2} \frac{A_1}{A_2} V_1$$

When evaluating this equation, additional information about density ρ_2 at streamtube discharge is required.

Example

$\rho_1 = \rho_2$ incompressible flow, i.e. density constant
$A_2 = 2A_1$ exhaust area twice that of inlet area

Result

$V_2 = \tfrac{1}{2}V_1$ exhaust velocity is half that of inlet velocity.

2.4.4   Conservation of energy

For an understanding of how a jet engine functions, conservation of energy is of paramount importance, together with a grasp of the law of mass conservation and the thrust equation. We chose as an example a section of a turbojet engine between combustion chamber inlet (station 3) and turbine discharge (station 5, **Fig 2-7**). This section was selected because heat of quantity Q is added to the gas in the combustion chamber, while mechanical work is extracted in the turbine, in the form of shaft power.

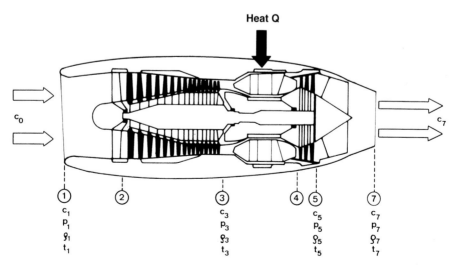

Fig 2-7   Explaining conservation of energy

The energy conservation law states that energy contained in the gas when entering the control volume, plus energy added or extracted within that control volume, equals the energy of the gas leaving the control volume. Energy cannot disappear.

When entering a control volume, the energy of the gas comprises the following components:

1 Internal energy, depending only on the temperature of the gas, expressed by thermodynamic quantities *specific heat at constant volume* c_v and static temperature t_3, i.e. $c_v t_3$
2 Pressure energy, expressed by static pressure p_3 and density ρ_3, i.e. p_3/ρ_3
3 Kinetic energy, expressed by the square of the gas velocity, i.e. $c_3^2/2$

In the combustion chamber heat Q is added. In cycle analysis, heat (of dimension $J = Nm/s$ in SI units) is usually referenced to mass flow rate (kg/s) to arrive at consistent dimensions, namely $Nm/s /kg/s = m^2/s^2$.

In a turbine mechanical energy is extracted which we may denote by l_t, also with dimension m^2/s^2 in SI units.

When the gas is leaving the control volume at turbine discharge (station 5), gas energy consists of the following components:

1 Internal energy $c_v t_5$
2 Pressure energy p_5/ρ_5
3 Kinetic energy $c_5^2/2$

The following energy balance may now be made:

$$c_v t_3 + \frac{p_3}{\rho_3} + \frac{c_3^2}{2} + \frac{Q}{\dot{m}} - l_t = c_v t_5 + \frac{p_5}{\rho_5} + \frac{c_5^2}{2}$$

Without going into further detail it should be noted that the above equation represents the *first law in thermodynamics*.

If neither heat is added to the gas nor mechanical work extracted from it, the energy equation will reduce to

$$h_3 + \frac{c_3^2}{2} = h_5 + \frac{c_5^2}{2}$$

We have denoted as *static enthalpy* h:

$$h = c_v t_s + p/\rho = c_p t_s$$

which together with kinetic energy $c^2/2$ forms total enthalpy H:

$$H = c_p t_s + \frac{c^2}{2} = c_p t_t$$

t_t is denoted as *total temperature* which will be frequently used in subsequent chapters, as well as total pressure p_t. Total quantities merely denote kinetic energy components added to their respective static values. Static quantities such as static pressure p_s or static temperature t_s are those which may be measured with hand-held instruments. In a jet engine where airflow quickly passes through, static quantities could be measured if instruments could be made to move with the fluid, i.e. without registering any velocity. Distinction between static and total quantities serves the better to understand jet engine functioning.

2.5   Engine performance parameters

Performance parameters which are of direct utility to the aircraft designer are *thrust* and *specific fuel consumption*.

Thrust
The most important parameter for engine classification is thrust (Chapter 2.3).
Thrust equation:

$$T = \dot{m}(c_9 - c_0) + (p_9 A_9 - p_0 A_0)$$

If the propulsive jet when discharging from the nozzle, is not expanding to atmospheric pressure, then at the exhaust nozzle cross section area A_9 a pressure force $A_9(p_9 - p_0)$ arises which is acting in the direction of the thrust. However, the maximum theoretical thrust will not be achievable in this case as the exhaust velocity cannot achieve its maximum, and the additional pressure force (although supporting thrust) cannot compensate the momentum deficit. Highest efficiency is obtained with the nozzle *adapted*, which would require $p_9 = p_0$.

Specific fuel consumption (SFC)
Next to thrust, specific fuel consumption is one of the most important engine performance parameters, defining the amount of fuel used to achieve one unit of thrust over a finite period of time. Specific fuel consumption is frequently given in the dimension of kg fuel/daN thrust/hour in SI units, or lbm fuel/lbf thrust/hour in British units, which are both of equivalent value.

Specific thrust
Assessment of how efficiently the airflow of the engine is converted to a propulsive force may be made by using a parameter which states how much thrust is achieved by one unit of mass flow rate. In SI units, specific thrust denotes the amount of thrust (in daN or kN) produced by 1 kg/s airflow:

$$T_{sp} = \frac{T}{\dot{m}} \text{ with dimension } \frac{Ns}{kg}$$

The specific thrust parameter may be conveniently used to compare jet engines.

Thrust related to frontal area
In order to characterize aerodynamic efficiency, this parameter relates thrust to the maximum cross-section of the engine:

$$\frac{T}{A_{max}}$$

Aerodynamic drag will increase with engine cross-section. Therefore keeping engine maximum diameter small is a prerequisite for an efficient engine installation.

2.6   Systems of units

Two systems of units pertaining to jet engines are in practical use today:
1 the International System of Units (SI system)
2 the British gravitational system of units
    The SI unit system (Système International d'Unités) is a standardized system of units adopted by all industrialized nations, though not yet fully implemented. Throughout the aviation industry other systems continue to exist, despite obvious shortcomings. Because of the greater familiarity of some readers with the British systems of units, examples and formulae will also be given in these systems, together with appropriate conversion procedures.

The International System of Units
This system was designed by Italian scientist Giorgi as early as 1901 and is considered the most modern of all systems used. It uses 6 independent units, of which four are of significance when dealing with jet engines:

the *kilogram* (kg) as the unit of mass

the *metre* (m) as the unit of length

the *second* as the unit of time

the *degree Kelvin* (K) as the unit of temperature

As units of mass, length and time are given, a unit of force cannot be chosen arbitrarily but is determined by Newton's second law (force = mass times acceleration). The unit of force selected was of such magnitude as to give 1 kg mass an acceleration of 1 m/s². This unit of force is termed a *Newton* ($1N = 1mkg/s^2$). This unit is too small to be convenient for denoting engine thrust. Therefore multiples of the unit are used: the Deka-Newton (1 daN = 10 N) or even more commonly the kilo-Newton kN (1 kN = 1000 N). Other units of measurement such as pressure, energy, power are derived likewise (**Table 2-1**).

The British system of units
Accepted units of the English gravitational system (EGS) are

- the *foot* as the unit of length
- the *pound mass* (lbm) as the unit of mass
- the *slug* as the unit of mass
- the *pound* (lb) as the unit of force
- the *second* (s) as the unit of time
- the *degree Rankine* (°R) as the unit of temperature

It is particularly important to keep in mind that 1 lb of force is defined as the force of gravity acting on a mass of 1 pound (lbm). Hence, 1 lb of mass corresponds to 1 pound of weight. For the frequently used engine performance parameter of *thrust specific fuel consumption* (TSFC), defined as pound mass of fuel per hour per pound of thrust, this quantitatively may be regarded as pounds weight of fuel per hour per pound of thrust:

$$TSFC = \frac{\text{pounds of fuel weight flow per hour, lb/h}}{\text{pounds of engine thrust, lb}}$$

Quantity	Unit	Definition
force	Newton, N	$1N = 1\dfrac{m \ kg}{s^2}$
energy/ work	Joule, J	$1 J = 1 Nm = 1\dfrac{m^2 kg}{s^2}$
power	Watt, W	$1 W = 1\dfrac{J}{s} = 1\dfrac{m^2 kg}{s^3}$
pressure	Pascal, Pa	$1Pa = \dfrac{1N}{m^2}$

Table 2-1

Also, *specific thrust*, another engine performance parameter defined as pounds of thrust per pound of mass airflow per second, may be regarded as pounds of thrust per pound of airflow weight per second, having the same numerical value:

$$T_S = \frac{\text{pounds of engine thrust, lb}}{\text{pounds weight airflow per second, lb/s}} = s$$

Conversion between both systems is provided in **Table 2-1**.

3 Air intakes

In the following chapters we will learn about the five major turbomachinery components of a jet engine: air intake, compressor, combustion chamber, turbine and exhaust section. Each of these contributes uniquely to the generation of thrust.

Because the airflow first passes through the air intake when approaching the engine, it makes sense to start our description with this section. It soon becomes apparent that this relatively simple looking component poses a number of fluid flow and mechanical problems. In some supersonic aircraft, for example, the air intake becomes an extremely complex device requiring enormous effort properly to control the airflow to the engine.

In any application – subsonic transport or supersonic fighter – the air intake is essentially a fluid flow duct whose task is to process the airflow in a way that ensures the engine functions properly to generate thrust.

Depending on engine arrangement and aircraft design speed, a great variety of intake shapes exist. Due to the influence of intake flow on overall aircraft performance, responsibility for intake design rests with the aircraft manufacturer, not the engine maker. However, both partners work closely together to arrive at an optimum solution.

The intake must be designed to provide the appropriate amount of airflow required by the engine and, furthermore, that this flow when leaving the intake section to enter the compressor will be uniform, stable, and of high quality. These conditions must be met not only during all phases of flight, but also on the ground, with the aircraft at rest and the engine demanding maximum thrust prior to take-off. Good intake design is therefore a prerequisite if installed engine performance is to come close to performance figures obtained at the static test bench.

Intake design basically is accomplished by applying the laws of fluid dynamics. As the flow behaves differently at subsonic and supersonic flight speeds, a distinction is made between intakes that operate mainly in subsonic external flow and intakes that operate particularly well in supersonic flow.

3.1 Subsonic air intakes

The standard subsonic air intake has found widespread application with high-subsonic civil and military transport aircraft. Being of quasi-circular cross-section, the air intake forms the forward part of the engine nacelle. Subsonic air intakes are also applied to some combat aircraft and virtually all jet training aircraft that operate near the speed of sound. Here we find intake shapes of elliptical, half-circular, or even irregular cross-section, with intakes mounted on the fuselage sides or under the fuselage. An arrangement with the intake in the fuselage nose, as applied to the F-100 Super Sabre fighter of the fifties, for example, is no longer used because it requires a long duct extending for much of the length of the fuselage, entailing great fluid dynamic losses.

Flow problems associated with the air intake result from the extensive operating range of the engine, ranging from full thrust with the aircraft on the ground, up to cruising speed at altitude.

Of particular importance is the pre-take-off static case with the engine delivering maximum thrust. As the ambient air in this particular

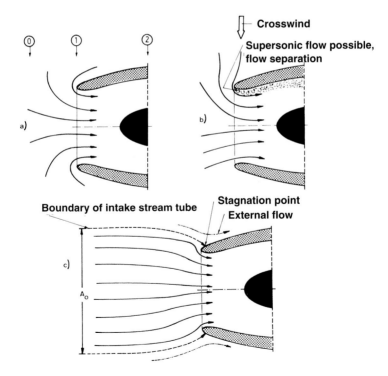

Fig 3-1   Intake flowfield
   a) aircraft at rest (static)
   b) static plus crosswind
   c) low-speed flight

case is nominally at rest, the air within the inlet duct must be accelerated to the velocity required by the compressor. In the static case the intake acts like a sink drain in that it has a core depression drawing in fluid. In the engine case the fluid is air, which is drawn from around the nacelle, even from behind the intake lip (**Fig 3-1a**). Airflow from behind the lip, in particular, is forced around the sharply-bent lip contour where the flow may separate due to extreme local acceleration. Separated flow entering the engine may, however, critically degrade engine performance. To reduce the risk of flow separation, the intake lip is well rounded which will always result in a thicker lip. On the other hand, high-speed performance requires thin intake lips, so large-radius intake lips must be avoided.

The idealized assumption of ambient air at rest and with ingestion into the intake uniformly from all sides is not to be found in practice. Due to the vicinity of aircraft components such as engine pylon, wing, and fuselage, deviations from the ideal will result which distort the airflow and degrade intake performance. Additionally, when engines are mounted under the wing, a ground vortex can develop which is swallowed by the intake and acts to degrade intake performance. Fortunately, this vortex disappears with the aircraft accelerating during the take-off run. With rear-mounted engines, a similar vortex develops on the fuselage which also disappears as the aircraft takes up speed. These vortices become visible if the runway is wet, or if atmospheric conditions favour condensation effects, and may be seen from the passenger cabin.

Another source of impairing intake performance is crosswind. On the windward side of the air intake, the crosswind component adds to the flow at the lip, leading to a further increase of excess velocity there (**Fig 3-1b**). If the crosswind is strong enough, velocity at the lip may even exceed the speed of sound locally, with separated flow entering the compressor. Because of possible blade damage, some aircraft are restricted from applying full thrust before the aircraft has attained a specific minimum ground rolling speed. This is the case, for example, with the Lockheed C5-A Galaxy, for which a 'rolling' take-off is required if the crosswind exceeds a velocity of 45 km/h (24 kt).

As the aircraft accelerates further during the ground roll, the streamline pattern at the air intake changes. Because air is no longer induced from downstream of the lip, disturbances from aircraft components in that area are largely eliminated. However, as long as the aircraft has not achieved a velocity suitable for the compressor, airflow will continue to be accelerated within the intake duct, though to a lesser degree. This fact is reflected by the streamtube pattern approaching the intake (**Fig 3-1c**). Because airflow within the streamtube corresponds to mass flow rate of the engine, a contraction of the streamtube will be observed, the bounding streamlines of which will terminate in stagnation points on the cowl. With aircraft velocity increasing, stagnation points continue to move forward on the cowl.

As cross section A_0 of the streamtube well ahead of the intake is determined by engine mass flow rate, the size of the streamtube may simply be determined by applying continuity considerations. Continuity requires mass flow rate $\dot{m}$ at any cross-section within the streamtube to be the same, which is hence a constant. Mass flow rate at cross-section A_0, in particular, exactly equals mass flow rate at the compressor face A_2, which itself reflects engine mass flow. Hence:

$$\dot{m}_0 = \dot{m}_2$$

We have learned in the preceding Chapter, that mass flow rate may also be expressed by air density ρ (Greek rho), airstream velocity V, and streamtube cross-section area A. Therefore, the requirement of mass conservation may be expressed for the particular flowpath stations 0 (upstream infinity) and 2 (compressor face) as follows:

station 0 (upstream infinity):

$$\dot{m}_0 = \rho_0 V_0 A_0$$

station 2 (compressor face):

$$\dot{m}_2 = \rho_2 V_2 A_2$$

As both mass flow rates are equal by definition, cross section of the streamtube at upstream infinity will result as a simple expression:

$$A_0 = \frac{\rho_2}{\rho_0} \frac{V_2}{V_0} A_2$$

If the assumption is made that air density will not change within the streamtube between stations 0 (upstream infinity) and 2 (compressor face), then streamtube cross-section A_0 depends only on aircraft flight speed V_0, because airstream velocity at the compressor face is determined by the compressor, with compressor entrance cross-section A_2 a constant by design. With these considerations in mind, the streamline pattern at high-speed cruising flight will be characterized by a cross-section area A_0 at upstream infinity, which is markedly smaller than the cross-section at the entrance of the intake (the intake 'highlight' area). This will result in a deceleration of the flow immediately upstream of the intake, with pressure increasing even before the airflow enters the intake (**Fig 3-2a**).

We have learned in the preceding paragraphs that for an airbreathing engine to function correctly, compression of air is a prerequisite. Aerodynamic compression occurs in flow ducts whose cross-sectional area gradually increases in streamwise direction. A duct

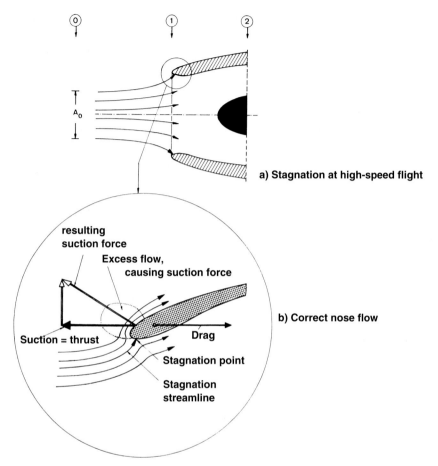

a) Stagnation at high-speed flight

b) Correct nose flow

Fig 3-2   Intake flowfield at high speed (cruise)
a) flow stagnating ahead of intake
b) ideal flow around intake nose

with the ability to retard a flow and convert its kinetic energy into pressure energy is termed a *diffuser*.

At sufficiently high flight Mach numbers, for instance at cruising flight, airflow approaching the engine will be faster than would be tolerable for the compressor. Due to the diffuser action of the air intake, which is a deceleration of the airflow and a build-up of pressure, airstream velocity will be adapted to the need of the compressor. Additionally, due to the rise in pressure, a considerable benefit to the engine cycle results so that less mechanical energy is required for compression. It should be noted that, in the case of a ramjet engine (which we will not consider here) the complete compression occurs within the intake duct, eliminating the need for a mechanical compressor.

A fluid is reluctant to flow through a duct of increasing pressure, much as water resists flowing uphill. In fact, a diffuser may be thought of as a pump with no moving parts that raises the pressure of the fluid it pumps. In order to prevent the flow from separating along the walls, the interior surface of the diffuser must be carefully shaped, and be smooth and unobstructed by steps or kinks, otherwise the sensitive boundary layer (between main stream and diffuser wall) may separate. This would result in a partial loss of kinetic energy and its conversion into unusable heat, a process termed *friction* which always results in a degradation of total pressure. If it were possible for the decelerating flow to convert all of its kinetic energy into pressure, then total pressure of the flow would remain constant and the so-called *pressure recovery* would be 100 per cent. Due to friction, which is inescapable with real flow (as opposed to idealised frictionless flow), a loss in total pressure will result. What matters is an appropriate design of the diffuser that minimizes these adverse effects. Expertise is also required because calculation methods are still insufficient, despite considerable progress in the field of computational fluid dynamics (CFD).

When considering the three characteristic intake flow cases of static, low-speed and high-speed, additional fluid dynamic effects must be taken into account that pertain to an optimum intake design. First, it should be noted that a nacelle causes aerodynamic drag, which accounts for about 3 per cent of total aircraft drag. Not only that, a nacelle contributes to aircraft weight. Both factors affect payload and range.

Economic requirements therefore dictate that the engine intake must be a low-drag, lightweight construction, that is carefully and exactly manufactured. Because many requirements are conflicting, the final intake design must necessarily be a compromise. The primary task of the intake, i.e. to provide a flow of high quality, must not be compromised.

The requirement for low-drag will primarily be imposed by the high-speed cruise case. Today's high-subsonic cruise flight Mach numbers, which are in the range of Mach 0.78 to 0.85, call for an intake design which features a relatively 'thin' intake, i.e. where the external dimension of the intake is not much greater than the internal diameter. This will result in a small nose radius, leading to a relatively thin-lipped air intake. The external flow surrounding the intake streamtube will effectively be prevented from developing undesirable excess velocities at the lip, minimizing the risk of flow separation with its corresponding increase in drag. What is more, if the external flow is made to pass the intake lip 'correctly', additional drag resulting from ram effect ahead of the intake may effectively be reduced. Such reduction is accomplished solely by the airstream flowing around the nose. As the flow follows the contour of the nose, excessive velocities can develop which may even attain (low) supersonic speeds. This will cause a zone of low pressure around the intake's circumference, leading to the exertion of an aerodynamic force with a component acting in the direction of engine thrust and termed *nose suction* (**Fig 3-2b**).

However beneficial a thin intake is for high-speed cruising flight, performance at take-off or even low-speed flight will be greatly degraded. Due to an alteration of the streamline pattern at these off-design flight phases, the strong curvature at the sharp nose will cause the flow to separate at the interior part of the intake lip. Appropriate design measures must be applied to prevent flow separation in these critical phases of flight, even at the expense of a reduced high-speed performance.

One of these measures calls for an increase of intake cross-section the better to match engine airflow demand at low-speed high-thrust engine settings. However, high-speed performance will inevitably be compromised. Additionally, curvature of the intake will have to be increased within the intake duct where the flow tends to separate. If not done correctly, sonic velocity may be reached by the intake flow at the 'throat' where the cross-section is smallest, causing blockage (the blockage effect is further discussed in the nozzle chapter).

Another measure which has proven effective, particularly with sharp-nosed high-speed intakes, was the introduction of additional secondary intake ducts that open at high-thrust, low-speed or take-off conditions. Driven by a pressure differential between intake duct and external flow, a number of spring-operated doors around the intake cowl open inward to give passage into secondary flow ducts which serve to increase the effective intake cross-section and, hence, the airflow. At the same time, flow through the main intake cross-section is reduced, with the additional benefit of preventing the primary airstream from attaining excess velocities. (This measure is no longer applied to modern commercial transport aircraft because of the increased compressor noise escaping through primary and secondary intake ducts.)

We will now look at two hardware examples that demonstrate the complexity of subsonic air intakes.

The first describes the intake of the Lockheed C-141 Starlifter military transport. This intake is particularly noteworthy because of its extremely short duct, denoted as 'zero-length inlet' by Lockheed, which enabled a lightweight construction of high aerodynamic performance (**Fig 3-3**). Due to its small radius, the intake lip is relatively sharp-edged which made necessary a secondary intake system that comes into effect at high airflow rates with the aircraft static, or at low

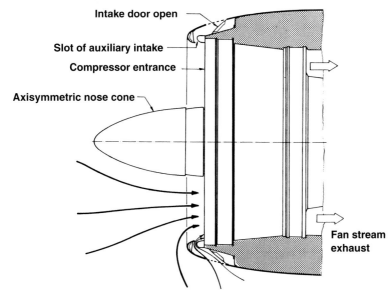

Fig 3-3   Air intake of Lockheed C-141

speed. The slotted inlet embodies 12 sets of outer doors pivoted at the cowl. The doors open against a spring force if a pressure drop exists between the low static pressure on the engine side of the doors relative to that of the external side of the doors. When the doors open, additional flow passages of nozzle shape (i.e. area decreasing in streamwise direction) are provided that terminate at the circumference of the intake duct ahead of the compressor face.

It is interesting to learn the reasons for designing a duct that short which so favourably contributes so little to the aircraft's weight. The answer is found in the requirements of the aircraft and the typical characteristics of the engine. The C-141 transport is designed to fly at around 430 kt (800 km/h) which is significantly lower than the speed of present-day subsonic transport aircraft flying at around 900 km/h (or Mach 0.85 at 11 km altitude). The Pratt & Whitney TF-33-P-7 engine, on the other hand, tolerates a relatively high compressor inlet velocity, not too far below free stream velocity. From what we have learned about the relationship of streamtube cross-section and airflow velocity, we may easily conclude that, in the case of C-141 aircraft, the streamtube cross-sectional area A_2 at the compressor face is only marginally greater than the streamtube cross-section A_0 upstream ahead of the intake. In other words, the crucial area ratio A_0/A_2 attains a fairly high value close to 1. Another benefit of the engine's high inlet velocity is the elimination of the need to decelerate the oncoming flow in the diffuser which would necessarily be accompanied by a reduction in aerodynamic efficiency due to fluid dynamic losses in the duct.

It should be noted, however, that the C-141 transport is a dated design that first flew in 1963 and entered service with the USAF in 1964. Similarly with the engines. The TF-33 engine's bypass-ratio of only 1.4:1 reflects the state-of-the-art of the early sixties. Present day engines feature bypass-ratios of 5 and more, with greatly improved performance. These engines require an intake that precludes a short-duct solution. Also, from noise considerations a short-duct inlet is less desirable. However, with the available technology of the time the intake of the C-141 constitutes an engineering masterpiece on which we can draw even today when seeking advanced engineering solutions with state-of-the-art hardware.

The second hardware example deals with the air intake of the Lockheed C-5 Galaxy military transport (**Fig 3-4**). The C-5 truly is considered the precursor of all modern wide-body civil transport airplanes of today. The C-5 is powered by four high bypass-ratio engines, the TF-39 from General Electric with a bypass-ratio of 8:1. First flight was in 1968 and entry into service with the USAF in 1969.

When investigating a zero-length intake design for the high

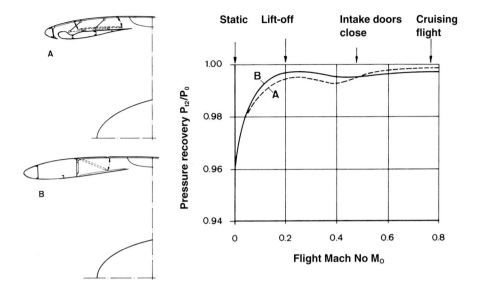

Fig 3-4   Air intake characteristics of Lockheed C-5A

bypass-ratio TF-39 engine, it became clear that the design (= cruising flight) streamtube cross-section ahead of the intake was much smaller than the frontal area of the big engine and this made impossible a practical version of such an intake. After intense studies to reduce intake length and weight, consistent with good low-speed performance, an intake design emerged featuring double-slotted auxiliary inlets that required only a single row of external doors. Instead of depressing at one end about a hinge line at the other (as on the C-141), these doors would open radially inwards exposing access to a pair of slots, one just forward of the inlet throat (where cross-section is smallest) and another at the diffuser exit (**Fig 3-4A**). This design reduced inlet length by 27% relative to the best competitive single-slotted inlet. In addition, inlet performance, both statically and during cruise, showed a significant improvement. Lift-off performance at Mach 0.2, however, was slightly inferior. Due to extreme sensitivity of the C-5 payload to take-off and ('second-segment') climb performance (with one engine inoperative), this intake design eventually had to be discarded.

The development program then focused on the question whether the advantages of a non-slotted intake as a simple, reliable and low-cost alternative, could be offset by the drag and weight savings of a single-slotted design. Detailed trade-offs showed that a nacelle with no slots would require a diameter of 2.74 m (108 in) compared to 2.60 m (102.5 in) if a single diffuser exit were selected. In the light of greater aerodynamic drag, increased frontal area and greater interference risk associated with the larger-diameter nacelle, the unslotted approach was eliminated in favour of the single-slotted shorter inlet (**Fig 3-4B**).

Again it should be noted that today's stringent low-noise requirements together with advances made in intake design have eliminated slotted intakes in present-day airliners. Nevertheless, the slotted intake was a remarkable step forward in matching the low-speed and high-speed airflow requirements of high-subsonic transport aircraft engines. It was also employed with early Boeing 747 airliners.

Intake figures-of-merit
The complexity of a subsonic air intake, as indicated by the examples given, obviously renders intake design an onerous task. In spite of tremendous advances made in the field of computational fluid dynamics, intake design remains essentially experimental, in particular when separating flow must be considered. For experiments, scaled intake models are investigated at different freestream velocities and airflow ratios (that correspond to engine settings). After a number of necessary modifications, the optimum intake configuration will be selected and investigated on a full-scale model. Due to possible size effects, modifications may nevertheless still be required.

In this context it is worthwhile discussing some of the criteria on which intake efficiency is judged.

One of the major figures-of-merit that describe intake efficiency is *pressure recovery*, defined as the ratio of total pressures at the compressor face, p_{t2}, and that of undisturbed flow ahead of the intake, p_{t0}:

Intake pressure recovery $\Pi_{intake} = p_{t2}/p_{t0}$

As total pressure is the sum both of static pressure, and dynamic pressure, the pressure recovery factor is a measure of how efficiently the kinetic energy of the intake flow is converted into pressure energy. Due to the friction of the airflow in contact with the intake walls, a loss in total pressure will always be present such that total pressure p_{t2} at the end of the intake (= entrance into the compressor or compressor face) is less than the freestream total pressure p_{t0}. The goal of good intake design is to minimize fluid losses by appropriate inlet duct and nose shaping in order to enable a pressure recovery factor as close to unity, i.e. 1, as possible.

The importance of the pressure recovery factor is demonstrated when reconsidering the intake of the Lockheed C-5A military transport (**Fig 3-4**). The shorter inlet with two auxiliary intake slots showed results that were distinctly superior to those of the single-slotted design both in the static and the high-speed operation. However, in the critical lift-off and second-segment climb regime (with one engine inoperative), inlet performance was inferior and it was finally decided to revert to the heavier single-slotted design.

Intake flow is not uniform at intake discharge cross-section. Zones of smaller or higher pressures develop across the exit, varying quickly both in position and intensity as the engine setting is changed. Therefore, the flowfield will always show some degree of *distortion* which degrades engine performance. In order to safeguard the engine against *surging* caused by distortion, a *distortion index* is prescribed by the manufacturer which the operator has to respect. Compressor blades may vibrate severely or even break when moving at high speed through a non-uniform flowfield. A widely used figure-of-merit that quantifies the degree of distortion to be tolerated by a particular engine, is the *DC60 parameter* which is determined from total pressure measurements within the intake (**Fig 3-5**). The DC60 parameter is defined as:

$$DC60 = \frac{p_{t,av} - p_{t,60min}}{q}$$

In this expression $p_{t,av}$ is the average total pressure at the intake as measured by a rake manometer which usually has six arms. The pressure $p_{t,60min}$ is also an average value that is defined as follows:

Along each of the rake's six arms a radial pressure distribution is measured by several pressure taps. For each of the radial pressure distributions the average is determined and plotted as a function of the circular arc position. Then a 60° wide sector is selected which shows the lowest total pressure and thus the highest fluid loss.

The difference of these two pressures gives the maximum deviation from an average and thus defines the DC60 parameter. Finally, because the DC60 parameter is non-dimensional, the difference has to be referenced to an averaged dynamic pressure yielded from static pressure measurements across the intake section.

As an example we consider the intake of the VFW 614 aircraft. For the M45H turbofan, the manufacturer, Rolls-Royce, had guaranteed surge-free engine operation if the DC60 parameter were less than 0.3. Intake distortion was measured in the wind tunnel using 6-armed rakes.

With these remarks we will conclude our short course on subsonic intakes. In the following chapters we will turn to supersonic intakes.

3.2   Supersonic flows

When a body is moving through air faster than the speed of sound, it will experience a different reaction from the air than that when flying at subsonic speed. In order to permit aircraft to fly at supersonic speeds, their shape has to be adapted to the peculiar characteristics of supersonic flow. This is particularly true for air intakes.

Before considering intake aerodynamics, a brief survey of the typical features of supersonic flows is desirable. A key to the understanding of such flows is a particular property of gas: *compressibility*. When a pressure is exerted upon a gas, more of the gas's molecules are packed into a given volume. A liquid, by contrast, is largely incompressible.

3.2.1   Speed of sound and Mach number

We assume that a sound-generating source will emit small pressure disturbances into the air, a spoken word for example. We know from experience that the propagation of a sound will take a recognizable interval. We see a lightning flash (= disturbance), but hear the sound of it (thunder) somewhat later. The velocity at which such pressure disturbances or sound waves travel in a fluid medium is termed the *speed of sound*. When considering air as the fluid medium, the speed of sound is seen to depend largely on absolute temperature t_t, and may easily be calculated:

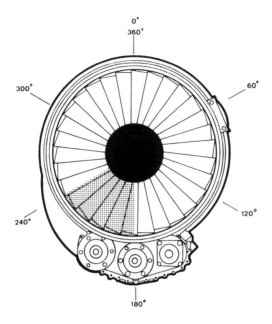

$$\text{Distortion parameter DC60} = \frac{P_m - P_{60min}}{q}$$

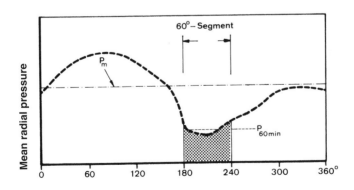

Fig 3-5   Explaining distortion factor

speed of sound a $= \sqrt{\kappa R t_t}$ m/s

$\kappa = c_p/c_v$ ratio of specific heats (see relevant textbooks)

R   gas constant, for air R = 287 J/kg K

t_t absolute temperature in degrees Kelvin, K

In the British system of units, the speed of sound is calculated likewise:

speed of sound a $= \sqrt{\kappa g R t_t}$

$\kappa = c_p/c_v$ ratio of specific heats (as before)

R   gas constant, for air R = 53.3 ft lb/lb °R

g   gravity constant, g = 32.17 ft/sec²

t_t total temperature in degrees Rankine, R
with t_t(°R) = t°F + 459

Fig 3-6 Pressure taps on rake of model intake and full-size intake

Example

a) Calculate the speed of sound at sea level for the Standard Atmosphere

Temperature of the Standard Atmosphere at sea level:
t = 15°C = 273 + 15 = 288K

speed of sound a = $\sqrt{1.4 \times 287 \times 288}$ = 340 m/s

Dimension consideration:

$$\sqrt{\frac{JK}{kgK}} \quad \sqrt{\frac{Nm}{J}} \quad \sqrt{\frac{mkg}{Ns^2}} = \sqrt{\frac{m^2}{s^2}} = \frac{m}{s}$$

British system:

Temperature at sea level: t = 59°F = 459 + 59 = 518°R

speed of sound: a = $\sqrt{1.4 \times 32.17 \times 53.3 \times 518}$ = 1115 ft/s

b) Calculate the speed of sound at 11 km altitude for the Standard Atmosphere

Temperature of the Standard Atmosphere at 11 km:
t = –56.5°C = 273 – 56.5 = 216.5K

speed of sound: a = $\sqrt{1.4 \times 287 \times 216.5}$ = 295 m/s

The same example in British units:

Temperature of the Standard Atmosphere at 36,089 ft (= 11 km):
t = 389.7R

speed of sound: a = $\sqrt{1.4 \times 32.17 \times 53.3 \times 389.7}$ = 967 ft/s

It can easily be seen that as temperature decreases with altitude, so the speed of sound also decreases.

Because of the interrelationship of pressure, density and temperature as manifested by the state equation of a perfect gas R * t = p/ρ, the gas constant R and temperature t in the expression for the speed of sound may be substituted by pressure p and density ρ (Greek rho). Thus the speed of sound may also be expressed by:

speed of sound a = $\sqrt{\kappa \frac{p}{\rho}}$

This expression for the speed of sound more clearly states the influence of the most important property of air when dealing with high speeds, namely that of compressibility, primarily being expressed through pressure and density. When an aircraft flies at low speed, compressibility effects are negligible; the air's density does not change appreciably as the air flows along the aircraft. If, however, the aircraft's speed is high enough, the air no longer behaves incompressibly. The result primarily is a marked increase in drag, but also in a different behaviour of the aircraft's handling qualities. A pilot, therefore, ought to know if his aircraft is likely to experience compressibility effects.

Because the property of air depends on altitude, flight speed alone is not a reliable indicator of compressibility effects. When referenced to the speed of sound, however, a unique measure of altitude effects on aircraft aerodynamics is provided. This ratio of airflow velocity and speed of sound is termed *Mach number*, in honour of Austrian physicist Ernst Mach (1838–1916):

$$\text{Mach number } M = \frac{\text{airflow velocity}}{\text{speed of sound}} \frac{V}{a}$$

Because Mach number is a ratio of two velocities, it has no dimension. Aircraft designed to fly only at subsonic speeds (practically all transport aircraft) therefore fly at Mach numbers lower than one ($M < 1$), whereas supersonic combat aircraft and the Concorde airliner are able to fly at Mach numbers exceeding one ($M > 1$).

3.2.2   Pressure waves in air

The basic difference in the phenomena associated with subsonic and supersonic flight speeds may be explained qualitatively by considering sound or pressure waves emanating at regular intervals from a hypothetical point source (**Fig 3-7**). If the source is not moving, sound waves propagate spherically in all directions at the speed of sound. When viewed as propagating in a planar manner, successive waves form expanding circles like waves from a stone dropped into water (**Fig 3-7a**).

Now consider the source to be moving (from left to right) through air at rest, at a speed less than the speed of sound, i.e. less than the propagation speed of the pressure waves emanating from that source (**Fig 3-7b**). The illustration depicts the momentary situation of the source at the position shown, together with waves generated when the source was at the appropriate position of its 'flight path' (marked 1 through 5). As the source travels at a velocity below the speed of sound, the wave front in the direction of flight is always ahead of the source. If therefore, an aircraft is approaching an observer at subsonic speed, it may not only be seen, but also heard by him.

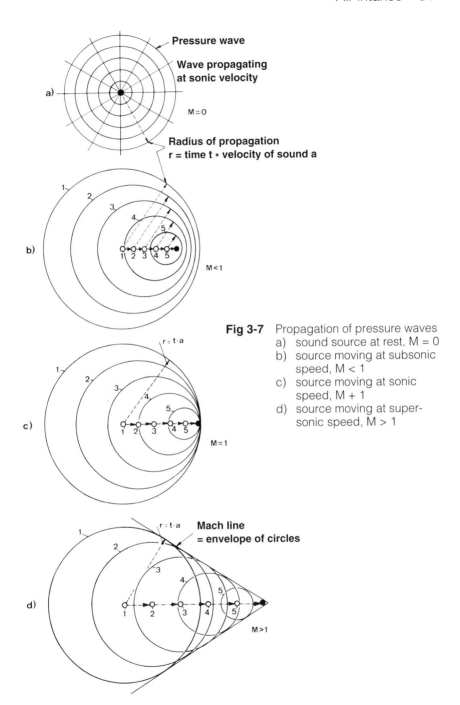

a) **Pressure wave**

Wave propagating at sonic velocity

$M = 0$

Radius of propagation
r = time t * velocity of sound a

b) $M < 1$

Fig 3-7 Propagation of pressure waves
a) sound source at rest, M = 0
b) source moving at subsonic speed, M < 1
c) source moving at sonic speed, M + 1
d) source moving at super-sonic speed, M > 1

c) $r = t \cdot a$ $M = 1$

d) $r = t \cdot a$ **Mach line**
= envelope of circles

$M > 1$

This will no longer be the case if the source travels exactly at the speed of sound (**Fig 3-7c**). An aircraft flying at Mach one competes in a race with the sound waves it produces. These waves aggregate into a strong wave front accompanying the aircraft. As the aircraft approaches an observer, it may be visible, but will not be audible to him until passing by with a roaring noise.

Now consider the case when the aircraft moves at a speed greater than the speed of sound, i.e. M > 1 (**Fig 3-7d**). All consecutive wave fronts it creates lag behind the aircraft and cannot overtake because of their slower speed. Consequently, in every successive position, an aircraft flying at supersonic velocity is outside and ahead of the wave fronts it has produced.

All wave fronts combined are enveloped by a conical surface, termed *Mach cone*, that travels with the aircraft. Any disturbance or sound wave produced is confined within the Mach cone. The half-angle of the cone is called *Mach angle*. The faster the aircraft flies, the smaller the Mach angle. In regions outside of the Mach cone, the air is unaffected by the aircraft's motion.

The foregoing discussion was intended to present basic concepts of supersonic flow phenomena in order to make aircraft behaviour at high velocities easier to comprehend.

3.2.3 Compression shock

Under certain conditions a compressible fluid like air may abruptly change its state. A typical example is the explosion wave.

Sound waves are considered small perturbations, that propagate at the speed of sound. However, abrupt perturbations associated with detonation waves may propagate at velocities considerably exceeding the speed of sound. Because of the large pressure gradient caused by such waves, they become audible as a *supersonic bang*, and the phenomenon is termed a *compression shockwave*. A familiar example is the *sonic boom* phenomenon caused by fast-flying aircraft.

Normal compression shock

Consider a fictitious tube in which a stream of air moves faster than the speed of sound, i.e. M > 1 (**Fig 3-8**). At some station of the tube a compression shockwave may have developed as a stationary wave front. We will now investigate how the state variables of the flow change across the shockwave.

The most remarkable effect that can be observed is a steep rise in (static) pressure ($p_2 > p_1$), coupled at the same time with an abrupt rise in density ($\rho_2 > \rho_1$), hence the term *compression shock*. The energy required to compress the flow is extracted from the kinetic energy which the airstream possessed upstream of the shock-

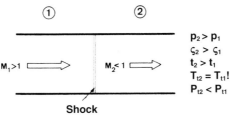

State variable	before / after shock	
pressure	p_1, P_{t1}	p_2, P_{t2}
temp	t_1, t_{t1}	t_2, t_{t2}
density	ς_1	ς_2

Fig 3-8   Normal compression shock

wave. As a result the airstream, when passing the shockfront, will abruptly decelerate. However, not all of the kinetic energy is converted into pressure energy. A considerable amount is turned into (unusable) heat, so that the static temperature is increased more than under idealized conditions ($t_2 > t_1$). In thermodynamic theory this is denoted as *isentropic* flow.

Contrary to the rising of static temperature across the shock, total temperature does not change, i.e. $t_{t2} = t_{t1}$. The reason is that the energy of the flow will remain constant if neither heat nor mechanical work are added to, or extracted from it. In other words, energy within a closed system cannot vanish. And total temperature represents energy.

The total energy of the flow is commonly expressed by two terms:

a)   its heat content (usually denoted as enthalpy) c_p t, which is equivalent to the sum of the interior energy c_v t caused by molecular motion plus the pressure energy of the flow, p/ρ.

b)   the kinetic energy of the flow, expressed by its velocity V as $V^2/2$.

If the flow is brought to complete rest such that V = 0, the kinetic energy will be converted to increase the enthalpy, which becomes total or stagnation enthalpy c_p t_t, formed by total or stagnation temperature t_t. This is a fictitious assumption, as the gas continues to flow across the shock, but the idea may serve better to understand energy phenomena. When passing the shockfront, pressure and density abruptly increase, also causing a rise in static temperature t and thus in heat content. At the same time, velocity and kinetic energy are decreasing. If no heat is allowed to escape, total temperature on both sides of the shock is equal (c_p t_{t1} = c_p t_{t2}).

Contrasting stagnation temperature characteristics discussed above, stagnation pressure will decrease as the flow passes a normal shock. We will remember that total pressure is made up of static pressure p and dynamic pressure $q = \frac{1}{2}\rho V^2$ (with ρ density, V velocity). Even if no heat is extracted from the flow, a heat exchange within the extremely thin shockwave will nevertheless take place, causing the decelerating process not to occur without, but rather with, the addition of heat. This, in turn, prevents the flow from attaining pressure and density levels possible without heat addition, a process similar to the flow within a diffuser, where heat due to friction loss is transmitted to the flow.

It should be noted that the amount of loss in total pressure increases with rise in Mach number ahead of the normal shock. This is of point when selecting the type of intake for a supersonic aircraft.

Another peculiarity of the normal compression shock is that:

a)   downstream of the shockwave the flow is always subsonic, whatever the velocity of the supersonic flow upstream of the shock, and

b)   the flow does not change direction across the shock.

Because of the sensitive reaction of jet engines to flow disturbances, a loss in total pressure is of major concern to the supersonic aircraft designer. This will be dealt with in subsequent sections. Before that, we will discuss how a supersonic flow can be decelerated more efficiently through an oblique compression shock, a method which is of major concern in supersonic intake design.

Oblique compression shock
A typical feature of the *normal shock* discussed previously is that the surface-like shock front is orientated normal (= perpendicular) to the flow direction, and the flow when passing the shockfront, does *not* change direction. In many practical cases, however, a supersonic flow will be forced to alter its direction, for example when approaching a wing, which by its mere physical presence effects a flow displacement. Where this happens, a shockwave will develop which is inclined at some angle with respect to the freestream direction. Such a shockwave is also formed if a gas, flowing at supersonic velocity alongside a wall, is forced to change direction at a convex corner (**Fig 3-9**). Because of the inclined orientation of the shock (as opposed to the perpendicular orientation of a normal shock) this shockwave is termed an *oblique compression shock*.

The main difference from the normal shock is a change in direction when the flow passes the shockfront. But otherwise the state variables of the gas (pressure, density, temperature etc) change similarly to the

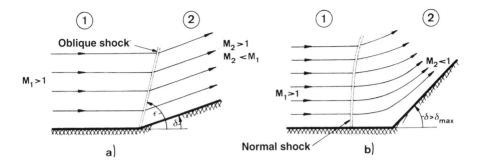

Fig 3-9   Supersonic corner flow
a) attached shockwave
b) detached shockwave

normal shock, although the changes are less severe in magnitude. In general, the intensity of the oblique shock is not as great as that of the normal shock, and likewise for the fluid dynamic loss. This is a major reason why the oblique shock concept is so attractive to the supersonic aircraft designer. Another characteristic of the oblique shock is that the flow in general stays supersonic across the shock although Mach number drops, i.e. $M_2 < M_1$ with both $M_2 > 1$ and $M_1 > 1$.

The inclination of the oblique shock cannot attain any arbitrary angle, because of a unique interdependence between freestream Mach number M_1 upstream of the shock and flow deviation angle. If the flow velocity drops below a minimum supersonic Mach number, or the flow deviation exceeds a maximum angle, then the conditions for the favourable oblique shock no longer exist. In this event the previously oblique shock instantaneously jumps upstream, changes character to become a normal compression shock, at least near the wall, with a considerable increase in flow losses (**Fig 3-9b**). The shock is then said to have *detached* as opposed to being *attached* if oblique shock conditions are met.

3.2.4   Supersonic flow over wedge and cone

In the design of supersonic air intakes, flow conditions over wedge and cone are of the greatest importance, as these are simple geometric bodies and relatively easy to manufacture. Let us first consider supersonic flow over a wedge. Such a device is installed in the air intakes of the majority of modern supersonic combat aircraft such as the F-15, F-14, MiG-29, Su-27, but also in the supersonic airliner Concorde.

We assume a wedge of unlimited length to be laterally immersed in a supersonic gas stream (**Fig 3-10a**). Flow conditions here are similar to the previously discussed corner flow where streamlines, after passing

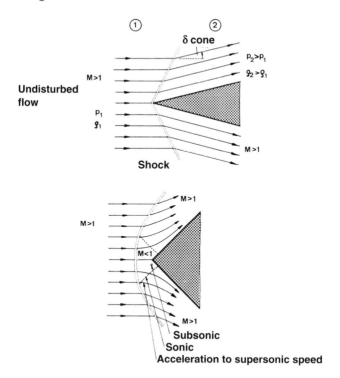

Fig 3-10   Supersonic flow over wedge
 a) attached shockwave
 b) detached shockwave

the shockfront, are everywhere tangent to the wedge cross-section. Due to the compressive effect of the shock, the streamline pattern downstream of the shock is more compact than it is upstream.

If the wedge angle exceeds the maximum value permissible for that particular Mach number, the oblique shock will no longer remain attached, but will jump abruptly upstream to form a (detached) *bow shock*. Part of the bow shock immediately ahead of the wedge apex acts like a normal shock causing the region between shock and wedge to be subsonic, i.e. M < 1 (**Fig 3-10b**). Adjacent regions of the shock surface bounding the centre normal shock region, increasingly bend in a downstream direction to form an oblique shock with, finally, degenerates into a (weak) Mach line (not shown).

Because shock strength grows as the shock inclination approaches the vertical, until a normal shock is attained at 90° to the direction of flow, i.e. zero inclination, wave drag increases accordingly. In order to design aircraft of low wave drag, the angle of the shock front must be small. This implies, apart from the supersonic Mach number flown,

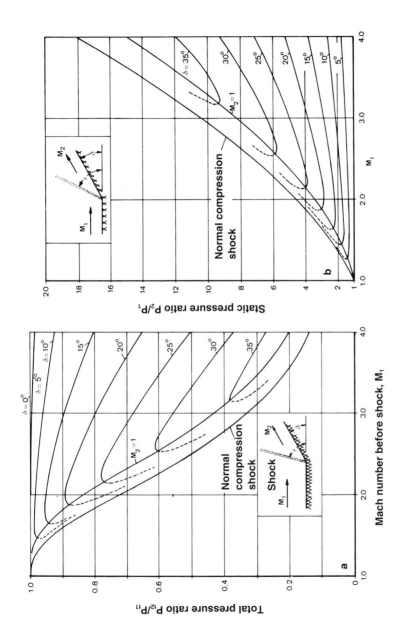

Fig 3-11 Total pressure loss and static pressure increase due to shockwave

that nose sections of intake and wing must be given a knife-edge shape. We now understand why subsonic intakes with their well-rounded nose sections are of less use in a supersonic flow: the detached bow shock creates high drag which will absorb much of the engine's thrust, so that supersonic flight speed is virtually unattainable.

The usual presentation of flow over a wedge is made on typical charts showing the variation of stagnation pressure or static pressure ratio across an oblique shock versus initial Mach number M_1, for various half-wedge angles (**Fig 3-11** left). Taking a 30° wedge as an example, i.e. a wedge of 15° half angle, total pressure loss at Mach 2 is only 5 per cent with the shock attached ($p_{t2}/p_{t1} = 0.95$), but 28 per cent with the shock detached ($p_{t2}/p_{t1} = 0.72$). On the other hand, the enormous increase of static pressure across a shock becomes apparent. Taking the same 15° half-wedge at Mach 2 as before, the pressure rise is twofold across an oblique shock, but five-fold across a normal shock (**Fig 3-11**).

So much for the wedge. We will now discuss conical flow, the second major design element of supersonic intakes. We will remember that when viewing streamlines over a wedge, their direction downstream of the shock is found to be parallel to the wedge surface at whatever section of an infinitely long wedge. Because wedge length is apparently of little significance in this basically three-dimensional flow, the flow over a wedge is frequently referred to as *two-dimensional*, which greatly simplifies the description of such flows. In contrast, flow over a cone is different.

First, some examples of practical application. Conical-flow diffusers may be found as a full cone in circular intakes such as on the American SR-71 high-speed reconnaissance aircraft, the Russian MiG-21, and the British Lightning; or as a sector of a cone in side-mounted inlets employed with the American F-104 Starfighter and French Mirage fighter which feature semi-cones; even a quarter-cone shape has proven possible with the American F-111 bomber. In general, however, aircraft with conical-flow intakes are all of dated design.

What once made the cone so attractive was its greater efficiency as indicated by its streamline pattern. After the flow has passed the conical shockfront where pressure abruptly increases, streamlines initially are not parallel to the cone surface (as over a wedge) but rather continue to follow a curved path, only to adopt a parallel pattern farther downstream. As long as streamlines get closer to one another, static pressure will rise. We thus observe a mechanism by which a supersonic flow is decelerated abruptly through a conical shockwave, and then further decelerated continuously until streamlines finally are parallel, with flow still supersonic (**Fig 3-12**).

The major advantage of a (supersonic) conical flow is a smaller total

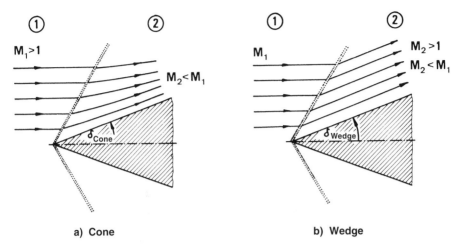

Fig 3-12   Comparison of supersonic flow over cone and wedge

pressure loss (when compared to a wedge of the same half-angle), together with the fact that a conical shock sustains lower Mach numbers until it becomes detached to form a high-loss bow shock. A major disadvantage of conical flow is that it is less tolerant of asymmetric flow conditions which cause distortion to the intake flow. As combat aircraft are frequently required to manoeuvre at higher angles-of-attack, the flow inevitably gets asymmetric – hence a preference for the (horizontally arranged) wedge in all modern combat aircraft, despite its reduced efficiency.

This brief introduction to some basic problems of high-speed aerodynamics may serve usefully as a basis for considering supersonic intakes in greater detail.

3.3 Supersonic air intakes

Appropriate design of the air intake is of the utmost importance to modern high-performance aircraft. Special attention must be paid to carefully arranging the intake to match the requirements of the engine. On the other hand, air intakes are fairly large aircraft components which require harmonic integration into the overall design of the aircraft so that aerodynamic efficiency is not impaired.

We will focus next on the internal aerodynamics of the intake, leaving aircraft/engine integration to be addressed elsewhere (see Chapter 11).

3.3.1 Intake configuration and operation

Present-day turbine aero-engines require subsonic flow at the entry to the compressor, even if the aircraft is flying at supersonic speed. The task of the air intake is therefore to decelerate the supersonic external flow to a subsonic speed acceptable to the compressor. As intake discharge Mach numbers are required to be in the range of Mach 0.4 to 0.7, great care must be exercised when decelerating the flow in order to keep total pressure losses to a minimum. Depending on the designed operating speed of the aircraft, different intake types are employed, their complexity increasing with Mach number.

For aircraft operating at a maximum speed equivalent to Mach 1.5, a *normal shock diffuser* is generally sufficient to decelerate the supersonic airflow efficiently to the speed needed by the compressor. This simple type diffuser does not require any sophisticated mechanism for adjusting the flow. At the design point of the diffuser, the normal shock is attached to the inlet lip, and maximum pressure recovery is stably attained (**Fig 3-13**). The action of diffusing, i.e. the deceleration of flow and build-up of pressure, is accomplished in two steps:

1. the supersonic flow is (abruptly) decelerated, through a normal shock, to subsonic velocity with an accompanying abrupt increase in static pressure;

2. in the diverging (subsonic) duct of the diffuser, where the flow is still faster than would be acceptable to the compressor, deceleration of the flow continues with pressure increasing further.

A characteristic of the *design point* for the intake is that the cross section of the *capture area* is a maximum, corresponding to the maximum airflow requirement of the engine. This condition applies to one particular flight Mach number and one particular altitude. If, for the same flight Mach number, the engine thrust setting is changed, by altering engine RPM, for example, then pressure at the compressor inlet (= intake discharge) will change accordingly and cause the upstream shock to change both position and type.

Suppose the airflow demand of the engine is reduced. Then static pressure p_2 at the compressor face will rise, less air is allowed to enter the intake, the excess airflow after being processed through the shock front is forced to flow outside the inlet as a so-called *spill-over* flow (**Fig 3-13b**). Since a normal shock causes a supersonic flow to become subsonic, that portion of the flow spilled over (and now subsonic) would have to merge with a supersonic environment, which would be physically unstable and thus unattainable with a normal shock attached. As a result, the shock itself becomes *detached* from the intake lip in order to find a more stable position farther upstream. In doing so, the central part of the shockfront continues to be of the normal shock type (which decelerates a flow from supersonic to subsonic

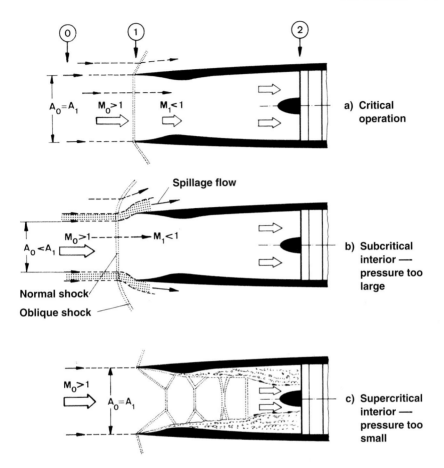

a) Critical operation

Spillage flow

b) Subcritical interior — pressure too large

Normal shock
Oblique shock

c) Supercritical interior — pressure too small

Fig 3-13   Operation of normal shock diffuser

speed). Adjacent regions of the shockfront, however, increasingly bend in a downstream direction to adopt the oblique-type shockwave whereby supersonic flow is maintained across the shock, with direction changing and Mach number reducing.

Now suppose the airflow demand of the engine to be greater than the intake can provide. At first, this is equivalent to a pressure drop at the compressor inlet, with pressure decreasing upstream, too. This will eventually cause the shock to be swallowed, and the airstream to enter the subsonic diffuser at supersonic velocity. The inconsistency of duct geometry and flow velocity results in a complex shockwave pattern within the duct which, together with a thick boundary layer due to flow separation at the duct walls, causes unacceptable flow to the engine –

a situation to be avoided during normal operation of the aircraft (**Fig 3-13c**).

A major disadvantage of the normal shock diffuser is a rapid reduction in efficiency as Mach number increases. The reason is that a normal shock incurs large total pressure losses even if the shock remains attached to the intake lip. This situation prompted the idea of conducting the supersonic to subsonic deceleration not in a single step (as by the normal shock), but by use of a number of less detrimental oblique shocks before terminating the supersonic deceleration by the unavoidable normal shock. The strength of the normal shock will then be weak enough to cause little loss.

An intake configuration able to provide such a staged supersonic deceleration will require either a wedge or a cone-shaped body suitably positioned within a subsonic diffuser. The number of oblique shocks will be determined by the number of corners at the contour of the wedge or cone (**Fig 3-14a**). The flow thus corresponds to the corner-flow type previously described. To what extent flow losses can be reduced by this method is shown by comparing two different supersonic diffusers at the same Mach number (**Fig 3-14c**).

By using a normal shock diffuser at Mach 2, for example, pressure recovery is only 70 per cent (i.e. $p_{t2}/p_{t0} = 0.7$), whereas with a multiple shock diffuser of three oblique shocks and one (terminating) normal shock, pressure recovery is 95 per cent ($p_{t2}/p_{t0} = 0.95$).

The operational characteristics of an oblique shock diffuser may be summarized in three typical conditions. If the normal shock that terminates the supersonic flow regime is exactly at the position of the diffuser *throat* (i.e. where the cross-section is a minimum), the airflow rate is a maximum (**Fig 3-15a**). This condition is denoted as *critical*. The inclination angle of the first oblique shockwave is then determined both by the freestream Mach number and the apex angle of wedge or cone. By axially translating a central cone, or by laterally pivoting the wedge surface at the apex, the oblique-shock may be adjusted so as always to be tangent to the outer part of the intake lip. Such a shock configuration assures acceptable intake efficiency and usually corresponds to the design point of the diffuser.

In the case of a pressure drop at the compressor face, the normal shock will be swallowed to adopt a quasi-stable position farther downstream within the intake duct (**Fig 3-15c**). This condition is denoted as *supercritical* and, due to the greater strength of the (terminating) normal shock, poor flow quality results.

Now, assume a rise in pressure at the compressor face such as caused by a reduced airflow demand of the engine. The normal shock will then be expelled from its throat position, and airflow is reduced. Intake operation in this case is *subcritical* (**Fig 3-15b**). Such a shock position

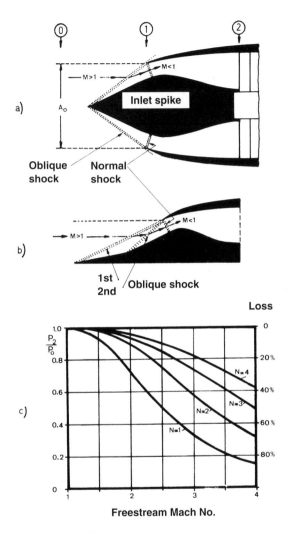

Fig 3-14   Multiple-shock diffuser
　　　　　a) twin-shock diffuser
　　　　　b) triple-shock diffuser
　　　　　c) Maximum total pressure recovery p_{t2}/p_{t0}

is highly unstable, the shock oscillating at a high rate between swallowed and expelled positions. This oscillating motion causes high-frequency pressure oscillations in the intake, known as *diffuser buzz* – a sound feared by pilots as it can indicate one of the most dangerous conditions of the propulsion system.

In a known case, a highly subcritical operation of the inlet (i.e. major

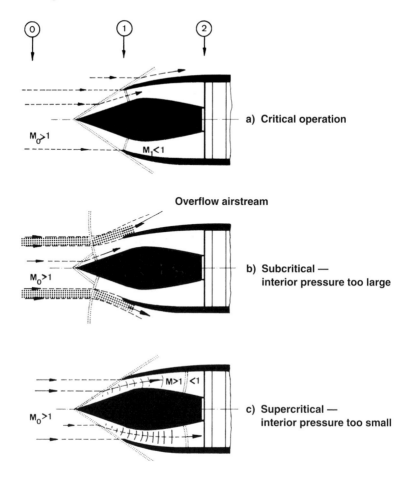

Fig 3-15   Characteristics of oblique-shock diffuser

excess flow spill-over) caused unstable diffuser flow extending down-stream into the combustion chamber where the flame was instantly extinguished. This in turn caused pressure in the diffuser duct to drop, the shock to be swallowed, and the fuel–air mixture to re-ignite. Rise in pressure thereupon caused the shock to be expelled again, and the process repeated. The pilot had no means of correcting the situation and the aircraft crashed. Such are the consequences that can result from flow anomalies in a supersonic intake.

3.3.2   Supersonic air intakes – case studies
An aircraft showing the typical application of a normal shock diffuser is the American F-16, now a product of Lockheed, but developed and originally built by the General Dynamics Corporation. The F-16's

Fig 3-16   F-16 combat aircraft featuring a normal shock diffuser

intake is of the fixed-geometry type, without movable parts – a decision made early in the design process to save costs. Provision was, however, made for the possible incorporation of a movable intake design at some later stage, but that appears unlikely ever to happen.

What is remarkable about this inlet is its positioning fairly well aft under the fuselage – a solution resulting from requirements of the aircraft. The F-16 was designed to have exceptional manoeuvrability and this required it to operate at high angles-of-attack. In these conditions the long fuselage forebody performs a shielding function which serves to align the airflow better with the (inclined) axis of the intake (**Fig 3-17a**). The intake itself features a short duct which not only contributes to the lightweight design of the aircraft, but also minimizes flow distortion ahead of the compressor.

Another problem facing combat aircraft is hot gas from gun muzzles that may be ingested and cause engine flame-out. By placing the gun muzzle above the leading-edge extension or strake, the high-temperature gas from the gun will be kept effectively away from the intake before being carried away by the external flow (**Fig 3-17a**).

However, this intake configuration is not beneficial in every aspect. The major disadvantage is that a normal shock system was employed which is less beneficial with regard to pressure recovery and maximum speed. Both factors were nevertheless deliberately accepted as the primary design goal was manoeuvrability, not speed.

Besides, more difficulties remained to be solved. One was the thickening of the boundary layer that develops at high angles-of-attack along the lower side of the fuselage forebody. In order to prevent low-energy flow from entering the engine, the intake had to be offset from the fuselage to free it from the boundary layer, which uninterruptedly passes along the fuselage.

The intake cowl features a moderately blunt lower lip that transitions into a sharp leading-edge extension or splitter plate on the upper side (close to the fuselage). The splitter plate extends 25 centimetres (10 in) ahead of the lower cowl lip to isolate the inlet normal shock from the fuselage boundary layer (**Fig 3-17b**). A short length of the splitter plate keeps boundary layer build-up small, so eliminating the need of boundary layer bleed on the splitter. The blunt lower cowl lip was selected to prevent lip flow separation and consequent flow distortion during aircraft manoeuvres at high angles-of-attack.

Similar reasons also lead the side intakes of the (once) YF-17 (now F-18) to feature blunt lips. The inlets are located under the leading-edge extensions to the front of the inner main wing. Large splitter plates separate the fuselage boundary layer from the intake flow, and then channel the low-energy boundary flow through wing root slots to the top of the aft fuselage, or along the bottom through a low-drag tunnel

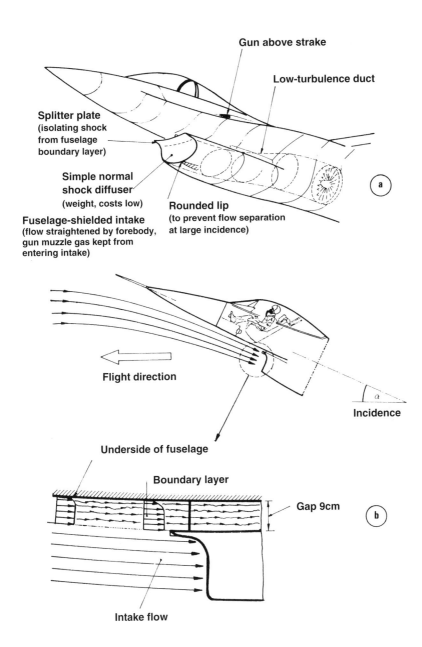

Gun above strake

Low-turbulence duct

Splitter plate
(isolating shock
from fuselage
boundary layer)

Simple normal
shock diffuser
(weight, costs low)

Rounded lip
(to prevent flow separation
at large incidence)

Fuselage-shielded intake
(flow straightened by forebody,
gun muzzle gas kept from
entering intake)

a

Flight direction

Incidence

α

Underside of fuselage

Boundary layer

Gap 9cm

b

Intake flow

Fig 3-17   Characteristics of F-16 normal shock diffuser

Fig 3-18   Lightweight fighter prototype YF-17 featuring normal-shock diffusers. Splitter plates on fuselage sides to keep fuselage boundary layer from entering intakes

between the engines. Newly-forming boundary layer on the splitter plates is bled off through numerous holes on the splitter just ahead of the intake.

Increased thrust levels available from new high-performance engines are demonstrated by both the F-16 and F-18, which easily achieve twice the speed of sound (Mach 2) despite employing higher-loss normal shock diffusers. Losses to the intake flow can be markedly reduced,

Fig 3-19 Multiple holes on the splitter plate ahead of intake to remove boundary layer of plate

Fig 3-20 Mirage III fighter featuring side-mounted oblique-shock diffusers

Fig 3-21   Axisymmetric oblique-shock diffuser (Lockheed SR-71)

however, with a two-shock diffuser as exemplified by the F-104 Starfighter, a famous airplane of the fifties. The same principle of aero-dynamic compression is also applied to French Mirage fighters which feature half-cones within their intake ducts. Side-mounted intakes are offset from the fuselage sides to prevent low-energy fuselage boundary layer from entering the intake duct. By axially translating half-cones, the shock position can be adapted to a changing flight Mach number. This process is controlled automatically through the air data computer to which a number of measured flow data are fed, such as dynamic pressure, static pressure, air temperature.

Only very few supersonic aircraft featured full-circle axisymmetric air intakes, examples being the Russian MiG-21 and the British Lightning fighters, both designs dating from the sixties. A prominent member of this group is also the American SR-71 from Lockheed, a high-altitude reconnaissance aircraft that flies at Mach 3. Also a design of the sixties, the aircraft was withdrawn from active service in 1993 on grounds of high cost, but three aircraft returned to flying status in 1994 after a serious gap in US reconnaissance capability was recognized.

Due to the extraordinary speed capability of this aircraft, noticeable also by its unusual shape, intake flow had to be carefully processed in order to make possible maximum performance. The unusual measures taken to arrive at this goal constitute a masterpiece of ingenuity well worth dealing with in more detail.

It will be remembered that, for the efficient deceleration of super-sonic flow, a multiple-shock diffuser is required because of its ability to process the intake flow through a number of oblique shocks, with a final terminating normal shock at the throat that transfers the flow from supersonic to subsonic speeds. Downstream of the throat, the subsonic flow is further diffused (= speed down, pressure up) to a lower Mach number as required by the compressor.

All supersonic diffusion must be accomplished by turning of the flow. With aircraft operating up to 'medium' flight Mach numbers (around Mach 2.2) supersonic diffusion is generally completed when the intake flow arrives at the cowl lip. As this process occurs outside the duct (i.e. over the cone), it is termed *external compression*.

At still greater supersonic speeds (Mach 2.5 and over) external compression alone proves increasingly inefficient because of the disproportionate rise in shock losses. Also, with an all-external compression inlet, the turning of the flow must be away from the inlet axis, leaving the flow at a high angle at the cowl lip. This in turn causes high aerodynamic drag of the cowl due to displacing the external flow, not to mention the difficulties of turning the internal flow back towards the engine.

A more efficient method is therefore to conduct only part of the supersonic diffusion as external compression, while the remaining part is accomplished within the intake duct as *internal compression*. This is achieved by means of a series of oblique shocks that reflect immediately downstream of the cowl lip as one oblique shock. By careful area variation in the ducting, supersonic diffusion continues in the supersonic passage of the inlet, terminating at the minimum cross-section of the inlet (throat) by means of a relatively weak normal shock (**Fig 3-22**).

The efficiency of external compression is further increased, and pressure recovery improved, by shaping the conical centrebody so as to generate multiple shocks rather than only one shock. This is achieved by giving the inlet centrebody a conical tip section, a slightly-bent middle section acting as a *conical-spike diffuser* to create a multiple-shock structure, and a conical end section, which together feature compression and non-compression zones.

Boundary layer on the spike is bled off through a porous section on the centrebody, near the throat of the inlet. Cowling boundary layer is bled off through a series of 'shock traps' consisting of 33 bypass tubes that channel this air into the bypass annulus of the nacelle and thence to the ejector.

Employing an axisymmetric diffuser proves beneficial as long as the

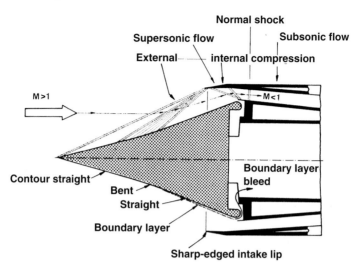

Fig 3-22   Mixed-compression inlet (Lockheed SR-71)

flow is aligned with the centrebody axis. Major disadvantages arise, however, if the direction of the flow is at an angle to the intake axis. Such a condition will occur during sideslipping or manoeuvring flight, and it may cause the engine compressor to operate dangerously close to the surge line, with flow distortion likely to occur (see Chapter 4).

In contrast, the two-dimensional diffuser is much more benign to non-symmetric flow conditions, even though at less favourable pressure recovery levels. A classical application of this type of diffuser can be found in the Northrop F-5 combat aircraft. The intake ramp is arranged vertically and slightly offset from the fuselage to avoid ingesting the boundary layer. Issuing from the sharp-edged ramp, an oblique shockwave will form as a standing wave, impinging on the intake cowl tangentially. This will, however, occur only if the aircraft is flying at its design Mach number. At off-design flight Mach numbers, for example when accelerating, the position of the shock is unfavourable because the velocity is transient and the shock not adjustable – a problem common to all types of fixed-geometry diffusers. In order to assist the diffuser to 'start' properly (i.e. to work as designed), numerous small holes are arranged in a pattern so as to constitute a perforated wall at the throat section. Porosity of the wall allows overpressure downstream of the shock to be reduced and thereby the risk of the intake to choke minimized.

Good efficiency of the fixed-geometry diffuser is achievable only within a narrow speed-band. A more flexible solution for adjusting

Fig 3-23   Northrop F-5 with vertical-ramp two-dimensional oblique-shock diffuser

intake geometry to a varying flight speed is provided by the *variable-geometry* diffuser. Hardware examples are the McDonnell Douglas F-4 Phantom combat aircraft with a vertical ramp diffuser and the Concorde supersonic transport with a horizontal ramp diffuser. Also of the horizontal ramp type is the diffuser of the US-Navy F-14 Tomcat fighter, the operating principle of which will now be discussed in some detail. **(Fig 3-25)**

Fig 3-24   Grumman F-14 featuring horizontal-ramp two-dimensional oblique-shock diffuser

In order to control airflow to the engines, ramps in the inlet duct are designed to pivot so as to alter the cross-section of the flow-path. During take-off and low-speed flight, the ramps are allowed to 'over-collapse' upwards, widening the throat area and so increasing the airflow without the need for auxiliary inlet doors on the sidewalls of the intake. **(Fig 3-25a)**

In supersonic flight, a combination of four shocks (three oblique, one normal) compress and decelerate the air for entrance to the subsonic duct **(Fig 3-25c)**. The first oblique shock is generated along the fixed-ramp leading edge, relative positions of the other shocks are controlled by variable ramps. The first movable ramp, hinged to the fixed ramp structure, carries the moving hinge for the second movable ramp. A third, aft-facing, ramp in the duct is hinged to the primary intake structure, and by its motion it forms the subsonic diffuser and the throat slot height. Ramp movement is automatically scheduled by Mach signals from the air data computer.

The bleed door on top of the intake is a two-position device which opens both at high angles-of-attack to preserve the engine stall margin, and at high speed to prevent engine 'buzz'.

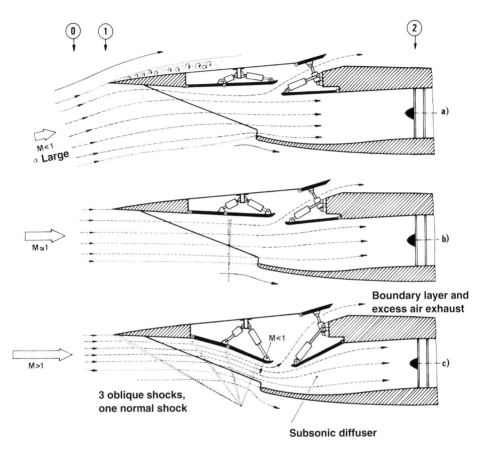

Fig 3-25 F-14 intake characteristics
a) subsonic flow at high angle-of-attack (manoeuvring flight)
b) transonic flow with normal shock emerging on ramp
c) External compression of supersonic flow through four shockwaves
(3 oblique shock plus terminating normal shock)

4 The compressor

In each category of a turbine-driven aero-engine – turbojet, turbofan, turboprop or turboshaft – the compressor is one of the most important components. It is the task of the compressor to increase the pressure of the airstream that is furnished by the air intake. This process is accomplished by supplying mechanical energy (= work) to the compressor, the rotating blades of which exert aerodynamic forces on the airflow. At the compressor outlet, a stream of highly compressed air is discharged to the combustion chamber, where more energy is added in the form of heat.

4.1 Compressor performance parameters

In a compressor, mechanical energy is converted into pressure energy. The amount of energy required, and the quality of achieved energy conversion, is characterized by compressor performance parameters. The most important parameters are:

- compressor efficiency

- compressor total pressure ratio

- air-flow rate

The *efficiency* parameter denotes the amount of energy supplied to the compressor from the turbine, by means of the rotor shaft, that results in an increase of pressure energy. This parameter, therefore, denotes the amount of loss that is always incurred by converting energy. Engine manufacturers exercise great efforts, both in research and manufacture, to keep losses as low as possible. Even the smallest efficiency improvements may become decisive in the selection of an engine by a customer.

Next, there is *compressor pressure ratio*. This parameter is defined as the ratio of the total pressure at compressor discharge (p_{t3}) and at compressor entry (p_{t2}), usually denoted by the Greek symbol Π (Pi):

$$\text{Compressor pressure ratio } \Pi = \frac{p_{t3}}{p_{t2}}$$

The importance of the compressor pressure ratio is because overall engine performance is influenced by this parameter as it bears directly on thrust, fuel consumption, engine efficiency. Engine weight, too, is directly related to pressure ratio. An increase in pressure ratio, for instance, may require the number of stages in the compressor to be increased, which will result in higher pressure and temperature levels within the gas generator. This in turn will necessitate a heavier engine overall because not only must the engine be re-designed to withstand the higher stress levels, but usually the combustion chamber and turbine as well.

The *mass flow rate* parameter denotes the airflow volume that the compressor is capable of processing within unit time, usually one second. Apart from the importance of this parameter for thermal cycle analysis, it also permits engine classification with respect to engine size to easily be made.

All three performance parameters are closely interrelated. Changing mass flow rate, for example, will directly influence pressure ratio and, in most cases, engine efficiency, too. Because parameters change with varying flight conditions, data given for engine classification are usually referenced to agreed standard conditions, such as zero flight speed, zero altitude, maximum thrust (see engine data in the appendix).

Present-day compressors achieve efficiencies of up to 90 per cent, compression ratios of 16:1 (30:1 with high bypass-ratio turbofan engines), and mass flow rates of up to 200 kg/s (up to 900 kg/s with high bypass-ratio turbofan engines).

4.2   Compressor types

Basically two types of compressors are in use, namely:
- the centrifugal-flow compressor, and
- the axial-flow compressor.

When engine technology was in its infancy (up to 1950) the radial-flow centrifugal compressor prevailed, both with Western and Soviet military fighter aircraft, although German combat aircraft of the Second World War utilized the axial-flow compressor. Today, centrifugal compressors are used only in small engines such as shaft engines for helicopters, auxiliary power units, turboprop engines, and some low-thrust engines for business aircraft. The majority of engines, however, employ the axial-flow compressor, this supremacy being a natural outcome of its ability to handle large mass flow rates, a prerequisite for the high thrust levels required by today's high-performance aircraft.

The designation given to the two different compressor types results from the direction of the flow relative to the compressor shaft axis. In a centrifugal compressor, the compressed air discharges radially outward, at 90 degrees to the spool axis, whereas in an axial-flow compressor the direction is parallel to the spool axis.

4.2.1   Centrifugal compressor

A centrifugal compressor basically consists of a rotating *impeller*, a fixed diffuser and a manifold which collects and turns the compressed air. Pressure ratio may be increased by arranging two single-face compressors in a row, which was successfully done with the Rolls-Royce Dart engine that powers, among others, the Fokker Friendship turboprop transport.

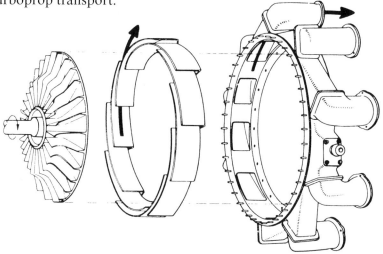

Fig 4-1   Components of a single-stage radial compressor

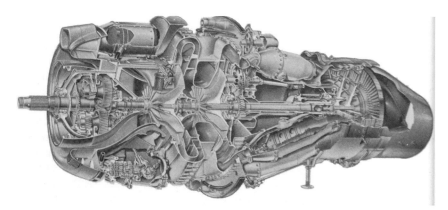

Fig 4-2   Turboprop engine Rolls-Royce Dart with two radial compressors arranged in tandem

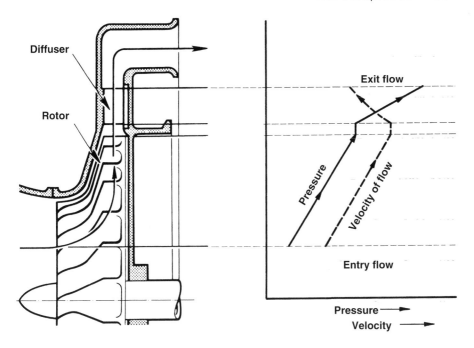

Fig 4-3   Pressure and velocity lapse in a centrifugal compressor

A derivative of the single-face compressor was the double-face compressor, which had a smaller diameter for a given airflow. Because of problems in supplying air to the rearward-facing impeller, and due to technical progress made to reduce engine size, this type of compressor is no longer used in aviation applications.

A major benefit of the centrifugal compressor is a large pressure ratio per stage (of the order of 5:1), and relatively low-cost manufacture – attractive features both for the small engine market and the automotive industry.

Operating principle
The impeller is driven by the turbine and revolves at high speed, usually of the order of 20,000 to 30,000 rpm, depending on engine size. At the entry to the impeller, near the hub, air is ingested and directed towards the outer circumference on the compressor by a series of inlet guide vanes (**Fig 4-3**). The airflow is induced by the high rotational speed of the impeller. This process not only causes the airflow to build up pressure, but at the same time to discharge from the impeller at high velocity. In the diffuser section, the kinetic energy of the high-velocity air is converted to pressure energy which results in a low-velocity, high-pressure airflow. The diffuser also serves both to straighten the flow

and to change its direction through 90 degrees to suit it for flowing through the manifold component. In practice, half of the pressure increase is accomplished in the impeller, the other half in the diffuser section (**Fig 4-3**).

Large increases in pressure are possible in a centrifugal compressor, typically of the order of 5:1, at an efficiency of 80%. Pressure ratio may be increased further by increasing rotational speed, but efficiency will deteriorate rapidly. The reason is that the circumferential velocity of the airflow discharging from the impeller will be supersonic and so cause shock waves to form within the diffuser, with attendant high losses.

Arranging two impellers in tandem, as in the vintage Rolls-Royce Dart engine, represents an intelligent engineering solution to increase pressure without exceeding the critical rotational speed. Less beneficial, however, is to turn the flow 180 degrees behind the first stage because it increases engine weight. Furthermore, turning the airflow so radically makes it prone to flow separation within the airflow passage that requires careful design in order to minimize losses.

4.2.2   Axial compressors

Most present-day turbo-engines for aircraft employ axial compressors. It was the axial compressor that made possible the modern generation of medium to high-thrust engines, and, in turn, the aircraft propelled by them.

The principal advantage of the axial compressor is its ability to deliver high mass flow rates together with large pressure ratios at the same time – features which the centrifugal compressor, due to is method of compression, cannot provide. The axial compressor is also beneficial:

– internally, because the air flows in a uniform direction which eliminates the need for turning the flow
– externally, because the smaller cross-section reduces aerodynamic drag of the engine nacelle.

The method of compression is different for each type of compressor. Whereas in a centrifugal compressor mechanical energy is transferred by means of *centrifugal* forces, in an axial-flow compressor energy is transferred by means of *aerodynamic* forces. However, because airflow in an axial compressor is diffusing (i.e. pressure up, velocity down), it is much more sensitive to flow perturbations. This must be taken into account when defining the operational envelope of such engines. Another disadvantage of the axial-flow compressor is its complex structure which greatly contributes to engine overall cost and weight.

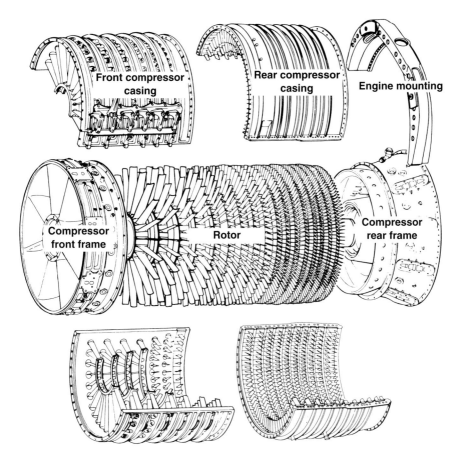

Fig 4-4   Axial compressor assembly (General Electric J79 turbojet)

Compressor construction
The axial compressor is usually made up of a large number of individual parts of diverse function. Although the variety of engine makes available on the market differ according to the requirements of individual applications, distinct types of components are typical to any compressor. These are **(Fig 4-4)**:

– compressor front frame

– compressor casing with stator vanes

– rotor with rotor blades

– compressor rear frame

Fig 4-5   Compressor front frame of General Electric J79 turbojet engine, seen from rear. Variable inlet guide vanes with trailing-edge exhaust exits for de-icing air

Compressor front frame

The airflow, after being delivered to the compressor face by the air intake duct, first passes the front frame. This is a ring-shaped single-piece lightweight structure made of aluminium alloy or steel, usually cast and then machined. Characteristic to this component is an outer ring, an inner hub and 6 to 8 streamlined supporting struts.

The task of the compressor front frame is to accommodate the rotor front bearing and to transfer rotor forces to the outer casing by means of the supporting struts. The aft facing flange of the front frame mates with the compressor casing to which it is tightly secured by bolts. The supporting struts are hollow to accommodate, for example, tubing to lubricate and ventilate the front bearing, and to provide space for electric cables where an electric starter is mounted forward of the shaft.

Power is also usually extracted from the compressor shaft to drive the accessories. This is done by means of an inner gearbox and a radial shaft, which runs through one of the radial struts to the engine bottom transfer gearbox connecting with the accessories. The interior of the hollow struts is also used as a warm air passage for de-icing the struts themselves.

Some engines feature movable inlet guide vanes downstream of the

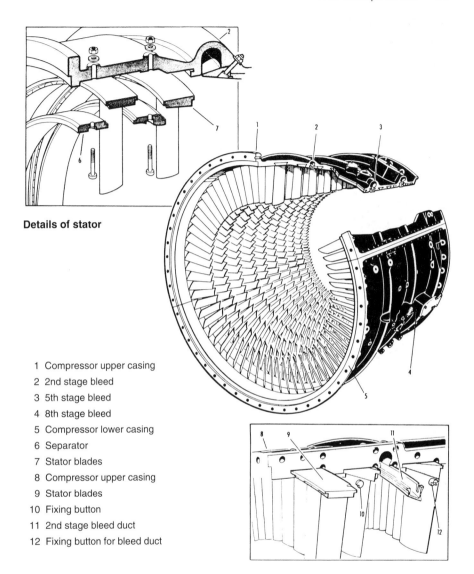

Details of stator

1 Compressor upper casing
2 2nd stage bleed
3 5th stage bleed
4 8th stage bleed
5 Compressor lower casing
6 Separator
7 Stator blades
8 Compressor upper casing
9 Stator blades
10 Fixing button
11 2nd stage bleed duct
12 Fixing button for bleed duct

Fig 4-6 Compressor casing (Orenda 14 turbojet)

supporting struts the better to align the flow to the rotating blades of the compressor. This may be essential if the engine is subjected to frequent changes in speed and altitude, as happens with combat aircraft. In the particular example of the General Electric J79 engine, guide vanes are hollow to allow hot air to pass through, which then exits at the trailing edges.

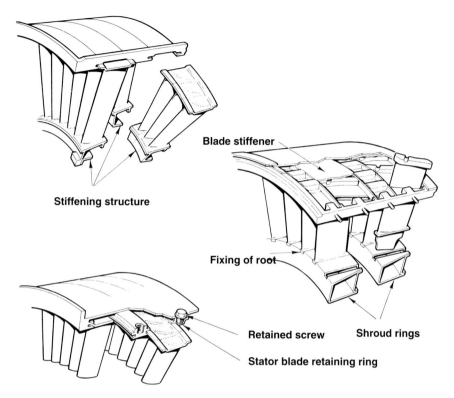

Fig 4-7 Stator blade securing to casing

Compressor casing

The compressor casing is a tube-like construction typically split length-wise to facilitate engine assembly and maintenance. After the rotor has been installed in the casing, both halves are bolted together through longitudinal flanges. Casing material is usually lightweight titanium forging, but stainless steel has also been used in the past. Modern high-performance engines employ alloy materials that were specifically developed to allow expansion of the case due to heating during engine operation, yet keeping rotor tip clearance margins acceptable. Such a material is the 'Thermax' alloy of Inconel, Corp. used in Pratt & Whitney's 4084 engine to power the Boeing 777.

The inner surfaces of the compressor casing are machined with circumferential T-section grooves to retain the stator blades. Modern engines also feature variable *inlet guide vanes* (IGV) to direct flow alignment. In this case variable vane bearing seats are formed by radial holes and counterbores through circumferential supporting ribs.

A proportion of the compressed (and thus heated) air is permanently bled, either through circumferentially arranged bleed manifolds or through hollow stator vanes. Bleed air is used for aircraft systems such as cabin pressurization and heating, wing leading-edge de-icing, and for electronic systems temperature control. The engine itself also requires bleed air both for de-icing the front frame support struts and nose cowl, and for cooling the turbine frame and blades.

Stator blades are locked in the compressor casing, either directly through T-grooves or by retaining rings. When secured directly, blades may be integrally shrouded at their tips to minimize flow losses. Longer blades in the front stages are frequently mounted in packs as a measure against blade vibration.

In compressors employing stator blade retaining rings, the blades usually have axial dovetail ends that fit into the rings. After each semi-circle ring has accepted its appropriate blades, the rings so prepared will be placed into the grooves of the casing and firmly locked in such a manner that they will not rotate around the casing.

Guide vanes are used to impose a desired direction to the flow, and to convert rotor exit swirl velocity into a static pressure rise. The number of guide vanes within a compressor assembly may be substantial, in some cases several hundred.

Rotor assembly
The rotor is considered the most complex component of the compressor assembly. Energies of several ten-thousands of horsepower may be processed in some compressors, in particular those of high

Fig 4-8 The casing assembly of a high-performance jet engine may hold several hundred stator blades (Stator of General Electric J79 engine, view from rear)

bypass-engines. Such severe load conditions require unique methods of rotor construction.

In its general design the rotor may be of the drum or disc type, or be a combination shaft and disc structure. In a disc-type rotor (which is the most common construction) the rotor blades are mounted on individual discs which are then separately secured to the rotor shaft, often divided by spacer rings. Individual construction varies with engine manufacturer, but the principle of transferring torque and axial loads at the same time is characteristic of any axial-flow rotor.

The shape of the rotor blades (like those of the stators) is comparable to a miniature wing featuring the typical aerofoil section. Unlike an aircraft wing, however, a rotor blade may be highly twisted from root to tip to obtain the optimum angle-of-attack to the flow everywhere along the blade length. The reason is that the root section travels much slower than the tip section and 'views' the flow from a different direction. The necessity for blade twist arises from the requirement for constant axial velocity being maintained across the flow path. The length of the blades decreases progressively downstream in the same proportion as the pressure increases.

Although out of production for decades, one example of a

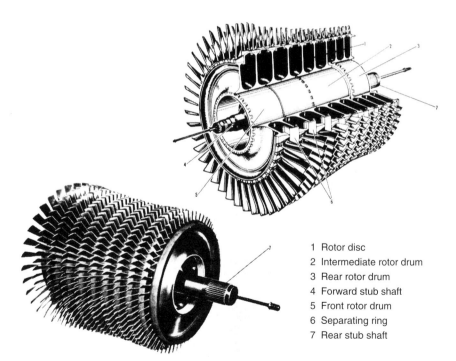

1 Rotor disc
2 Intermediate rotor drum
3 Rear rotor drum
4 Forward stub shaft
5 Front rotor drum
6 Separating ring
7 Rear stub shaft

Fig 4-9   Compressor rotor of the Orenda 14 turbojet engine

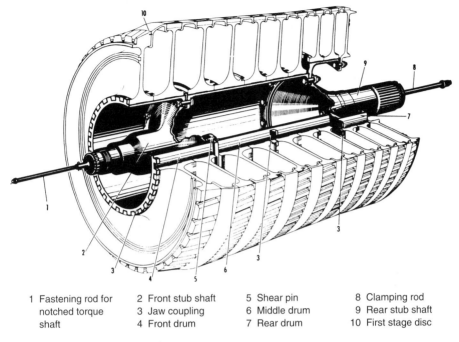

1 Fastening rod for notched torque shaft	2 Front stub shaft	5 Shear pin	8 Clamping rod
	3 Jaw coupling	6 Middle drum	9 Rear stub shaft
	4 Front drum	7 Rear drum	10 First stage disc

Fig 4-10 Drum rotor construction – a development of the fifties as a step towards the high-performance rotor of today (Orenda 14)

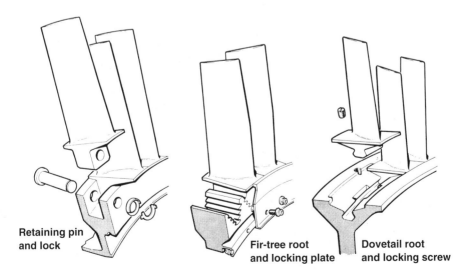

Retaining pin and lock

Fir-tree root and locking plate

Dovetail root and locking screw

Fig 4-11 Methods of securing rotor blades to disk

drum-type rotor may be useful in explaining the underlying principle (**Fig 4-9**). The engine is the Canadian Orenda 14, a veteran unit once used in the F-86 Sabre fighter of the fifties.

The drum of this engine consists of three elements which, together with two stub shafts, are joined by bolts to form a single unit (**Fig 4-10**). The connections are made with fitted bolts which transmit torque from the rear serrated stub shaft that connects to the turbine shaft.

Holding rotor blades in place while they transmit considerable loads has led to characteristic attachment methods of securing the blades to the rotor. Two types of blade root design are primarily used, *fir-tree* and *dovetail*, both of which permit blades to be firmly attached to the disc and still allow space for expansion during engine operation (**Fig 4-11**). The fir-tree base is of greater complexity and is used only where blade loading is high, whereas the simpler dovetail is now the more common base design. Dovetail bases may be of the axial type which are mainly used in the front stages, or of the circumferential type which is found more often in the high pressure stages. A simple yet effective method is to secure blades with fitted bolts, a method employed, for example, with the fan blades of the General Electric TF-34 engine.

Fig 4-12   Carefully checking the rotor during maintenance (Orenda 14 jet engine of the fifties)

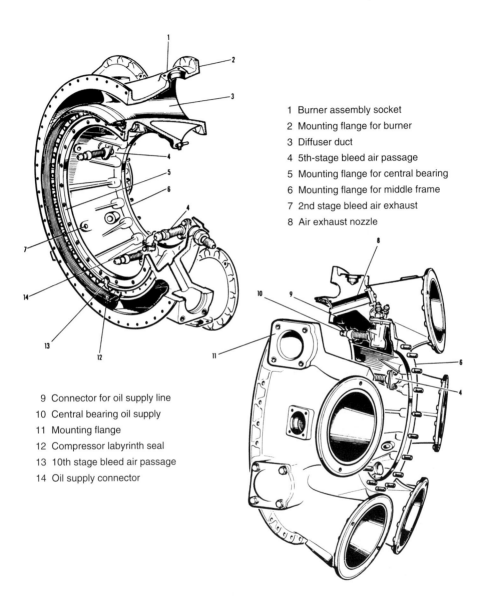

1 Burner assembly socket
2 Mounting flange for burner
3 Diffuser duct
4 5th-stage bleed air passage
5 Mounting flange for central bearing
6 Mounting flange for middle frame
7 2nd stage bleed air exhaust
8 Air exhaust nozzle

9 Connector for oil supply line
10 Central bearing oil supply
11 Mounting flange
12 Compressor labyrinth seal
13 10th stage bleed air passage
14 Oil supply connector

Fig 4-13 Compressor rear frame construction for engine with can-type combustors of the fifties (Orenda 14)

The long blades of the front stages are often free to move slightly in their seats, tightening up by centrifugal forces when the engine rotates. This method has been found useful in reducing stress concentrations near the blade root.

After final assembly the rotor must be carefully checked for proper balance.

Compressor rear frame
The basic airflow function of the compressor rear frame is to guide and deliver the pressurized airstream to the combustion section. Flow path design, therefore, reflects the type of combustor employed. When can-type combustion chambers were used, the flow path through the rear frame had to be equally apportioned to each combustor (**Fig 4-8**). The cross-section of the flow path progressively increases downstream to act as a diffuser, i.e. to reduce airstream velocity and increase pressure.

With regard to engine thrust forces, the compressor rear frame is of

Fig 4-14   Thrust bearings are heavy-duty components of a jet engine. Careful assembly of bearing in Rolls-Royce Olympus 593 engine for Concorde supersonic transport

great importance. In most cases it is here (or close by at the compressor casing) where the primary engine mounting is located and thrust forces are transmitted to the airframe.

The centre of the compressor rear frame is designed to house the rearward bearing of the rotor, a ball-bearing that absorbs the longitudinal thrust of the rotor. With high-thrust engines this bearing must withstand extreme loads.

The struts of the compressor rear frame, in addition to contributing structural strength to the compressor assembly, may also serve to facilitate lubrication and venting of the bearing as well as the supply of bleed air.

4.3   Compressor stage operation

Axial compressors typically contain between 8 and 16 stages. An exception is the fan of a high bypass-ratio engine which may be considered as a single-stage compressor.

A *stage* is the term given to a particular turbo-machinery unit in the compressor or the turbine. In the compressor, a stage consists of a rotor wheel carrying rotating blades, followed by a stator assembly carrying stationary blades or vanes (**Fig 4-15**). Upstream of the first stage proper a stator assembly may be used to provide optimum flow direction for the first rotor wheel, with vane incidence made adjustable to allow for different thrust settings.

The operation of a stage is most readily visualized by considering the flow at some midspan blade station, usually in the middle between hub and tip. Conceptual unwrapping of this 'middle section' results in an array of aerofoils representing rotor and stator blades and termed a *cascade* (**Fig 4-15**, centre). Investigation of stage aerodynamics is usually carried out in a cascade tunnel, an experimental setup where single or multi-stage cascades are tested under simulated flow conditions.

For study purposes flow in a cascade is considered to be largely two-dimensional, whereas in an actual compressor three-dimensional effects occur. Before going into detail of cascade flow, however, we will consider flow velocity nomenclature for a rotating wheel.

The flow when approaching a rotating blade at some (absolute) velocity V will be viewed by the blade as approaching at some relative velocity V_{rel}, because the blade itself rotates at a circumferential velocity U. Distinction must therefore be made between these three velocities:

1 *Absolute* velocity V as 'seen' by an external observer standing next to the engine.

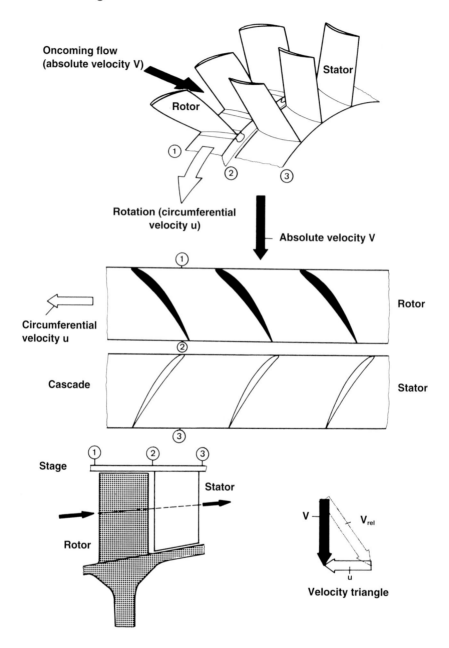

Fig 4-15   Compressor stage

2 *Circumferential* velocity U, depending on rotational speed (rpm) and radial position.
3 *Relative* velocity V_{rel} as seen by an observer 'sitting' on the rotating blade and moving with it.

All three velocities may be combined into a velocity triangle, or equally, the absolute velocity V can be assumed to consist of a circumferential and a relative velocity component. Because velocities not only have a magnitude but also a direction, they may be expressed as vectors, i.e. arrows of a length corresponding to their respective velocity, and pointing in the direction of the flow (for example: 1 cm = 100 m/s; *cf* **Fig 4-15,** bottom right).

We are now sufficiently briefed to comprehend the compression

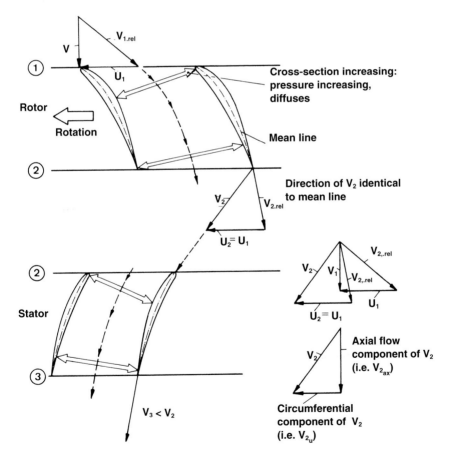

Fig 4-16   Flow and velocity components within a stage

process within a stage. Consider the flow approaching a rotor aerofoil at absolute velocity V_1 (**Fig 4-16**). The energy content of the flow is determined by the static pressure p_1, static temperature t_1 and kinetic energy $\frac{V_1^2}{2}$.

Together with circumferential velocity U (which depends on engine rpm) relative velocity $V_{1,rel}$ results, with a direction corresponding to the rotor blade mean line. With these components the velocity triangle at the entry station of the rotor is known (which we denote as station number 1, hence subscript 1, *cf* **Fig 4-16**).

Because there is an increase in flowpath cross-sectional area between adjacent rotor blades downstream, a diffusing action results and causes relative velocity to decrease and pressure to increase. (We thus observe the very same principle of diffusion already discussed in Chapter 3, Air intakes.)

The flow exits the rotor at relative velocity $V_{2,rel}$ which is smaller than $V_{1,rel}$ at rotor entry (hence the term *retarding cascade*). Direction of exit velocity $V_{2,rel}$ corresponds to the mean line slope of the blade trailing edge (**Fig 4-16**). Together with circumferential velocity U, the velocity triangle at rotor exit can be drawn to yield absolute velocity V_2.

What is noteworthy here when comparing absolute velocities V_2 and V_1, is the marked change in flow direction imposed on the flow by the rotating blade. This change in direction results from the momentum which the rotating blade has imparted to the flow as a direct input from the torque of the rotor shaft. The energy that has been transferred to the flow causes a swirling motion at the rotor exit and a change of the state variables of the flow (i.e. higher values of pressure p_2, temperature t_2, absolute velocity V_2 and kinetic energy $\frac{V_2^2}{2}$).

In this energetic state the swirling flow enters the stator assembly. Direction of flow velocity V_2 should, ideally, coincide with the mean line slope of the stator blade. As the stator blades are fixed and not rotating, there is no relative velocity and no energy transfer. Again, because flowpath area between stator blades is increasing, a further decrease in velocity results together with an increase of pressure. This is a self-sustained mechanism driven by the kinetic energy contained in the flow. Since kinetic energy is converted to pressure energy, total energy (apart from flow losses) will remain constant in the stator section of a stage. The rise in pressure is complemented by the drop in velocity so that the absolute velocity V_3 at stator exit is less than V_2 at stator entry, with swirl ideally removed from the flow.

Flow conditions at the stator exit of a particular stage constitute the rotor entry conditions of its successive stage. Because the maximum pressure rise possible with a single stage is only 20 to 30 per cent (corresponding to a pressure ratio of 1.2 to 1.3 per stage) a multi-stage compressor is required to boost pressure to a ratio of, say, 15.

After discharging from the last stage, the pressurized air will ideally be free from swirl and ready for the combustion process. If, however, the flow is still found to possess unacceptable levels of swirl, more vanes can be added in a second, or even third, row the better to turn the flow in an axial direction. With only one vane, separation of the flow may occur.

Bearing in mind that the energy transmitted by the compressor results in a change of the gas parameters, a simplified example may serve to demonstrate the enormous amounts of power required by a compressor.

At compressor discharge (engine station 3), the total energy of the flow consists of two components:

1   static enthalpy (= energy) $h_3 = c_p t_3$, largely influenced by the gas temperature;

2   kinetic energy $\dfrac{V_3^2}{2}$

Both terms may be combined to form total enthalpy

$$H_3 = c_p t_{t3} = c_p t_3 + \frac{V_3^2}{2}$$

(with t_{t3} = total temperature, c_p = specific heat at constant pressure, cf relevant physics textbooks.)

From total enthalpy H_3 at compressor discharge, total enthalpy

$$H_2 = c_p t_2 + \frac{V_2^2}{2} = c_p t_{t2}$$

at compressor entry must be deducted, because this was the energy the flow had possessed before. This yields specific compressor work (related to unit mass flow rate, i.e. 1 kg/s air):

$$H_c = c_p (t_{t3} - t_{t2})$$

Using the simple transposition

$$c_p (t_{t3} - t_{t2}) = c_p t_{t2} \left(\frac{t_{t3}}{t_{t2}} - 1 \right)$$

and the so-called 'isentropic relation'

$$\frac{t_{t3}}{t_{t2}} = \left(\frac{p_{t3}}{p_{t2}} \right)^{\frac{\kappa-1}{\kappa}}$$

ideal compressor work $H_{c,is}$ results:

$$H_{c,is} = c_p t_{t2} \left[\left(\frac{p_{t3}}{p_{t2}} \right)^{\frac{\kappa-1}{\kappa}} - 1 \right]$$

Example: Calculate the power requirement of a compressor having the following characteristics:

compression ratio $\dfrac{p_{t3}}{p_{t2}} = 10$

mass flow rate $\dot{m} = 50$ kg/s

compressor entry temperature $t_{t2} = 288K$ (15°C)

$H_{c,is} = 1.004 \times 288 \times 50 \times [10^{0.285} - 1] = 13{,}410$ kW

Dimension: $\dfrac{kJK}{kgK} \times \dfrac{kg}{s} = kW$

In a compressor efficiency is always degraded by the losses due to clearances between rotating blades and the casing. This is accounted for by an efficiency factor defining the amount of pressure energy actually obtained in relation to work expended:

compressor efficiency $\eta_c = \dfrac{\text{pressure energy available}}{\text{mechanical work expended}}$

In axial compressors efficiencies of 85–90 per cent are achievable, whereas in radial compressors the efficiency is less. Assuming an efficiency of 85% in the above example, i.e. $\eta_c = 0.85$, compressor power required is:

$H_c = \dfrac{H_{c,is}}{\eta_c} = 15{,}776$ kW

Using the more popular, yet obsolete horsepower conversion of

1 kW = 1.31 hp

yields $H_c = 20{,}667$ hp.

This example clearly demonstrates the enormous power required by this typical compressor. The power requirements of compressors used in modern high bypass-ratio fan engines with mass flow ratios of the order of 900 kg/s is very much greater.

4.4   Compressor characteristics

A compressor is usually designed to meet the requirements for one particular flight condition, manifested by a specific flight Mach number and a specific flight altitude (for example: Mach number $M_0 = 0.84$, altitude H = 11 km (36,100 ft)). This condition is termed the *design point*, where compressor performance must meet design requirements with regard to mass flow rate, pressure ratio, and efficiency. Additionally, however, the compressor will also be required to perform adequately at lower rotational speeds, which is termed *off-design performance*.

Engine off-design behaviour is particularly important when the aircraft is on the landing approach, with glidepath controlled by rapid changes of engine thrust. Another condition where off-design behaviour is of point is engine starting. Engine flow must be stable enough to allow for fast acceleration.

Compressor characteristics are derived from experimental testing in a specially designed test facility that allows airflow to be varied while the compressor rotates at constant rpm. Mass flow rate will be controlled by varying the exhaust cross-section, usually with a cone that moves in and out axially.

A compressor operating curve is obtained at a constant rotational speed N by measuring the following quantities:

- total pressure Pt_2 at compressor entry

- total pressure Pt_3 at compressor discharge

- mass flow rate ṁ (by using the pressure and temperature data of the entrained air);

- efficiency factor.

Testing usually starts with the discharge nozzle fully open to allow maximum airflow to the compressor (**Fig 4-17**, point 1). By stepwise moving the translatable exit plug closer to the nozzle discharge, airflow rate will be reduced and pressure increased. Drawing a line through all points so obtained will provide a *speed curve* on which rotational speed N is constant everywhere.

The rise in pressure by gradually blocking the exit section has a limit. A condition will suddenly be reached at which further blocking causes only minor pressure gains, indicated by the flattening of the speed curve slope until, finally, pressure begins to decline as blockage is increased further. The flow then stalls at the compressor blades, and the compressor is said to *surge*.

In practice, engine surge must be avoided because it can destroy the engine. A means of determining the operating limit of the engine is given by the first occurrence of compressor surge.

Additional test runs are made at different constant speeds, each of which will yield another speed curve, until the complete speed range is covered (**Fig 4-18**). Connecting the points on each speed curve where compressor surge is just avoided, defines the limit of compressor operation, the *surge line*.

Points of constant compressor efficiency form another set of curves,

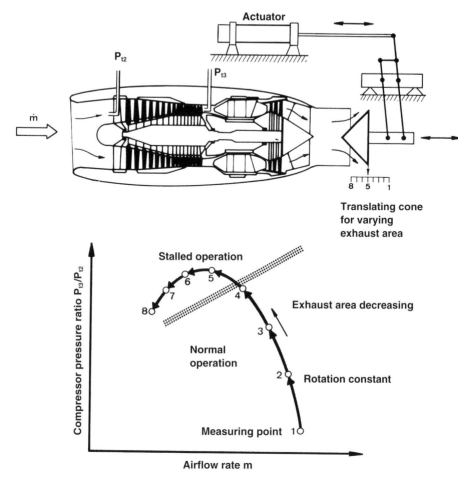

Fig 4-17   Compressor speed curve

the *efficiency lines* of typically elliptic shape. Efficiency is highest on the inner curve.

The parameters discussed above are used in constructing the *compressor performance map*. Data on such a map is not presented as measured, but is corrected to a practical form. The reason for the correction is that it is impractical to accumulate experimental data for the bewildering number of possible operating conditions, or to account for data obtained at different facilities. A solution whereby the data mass is brought into a form that is universally valid comes from 'dimensional analysis', a mathematical method which has provided many useful non-dimensional or modified performance parameters that are

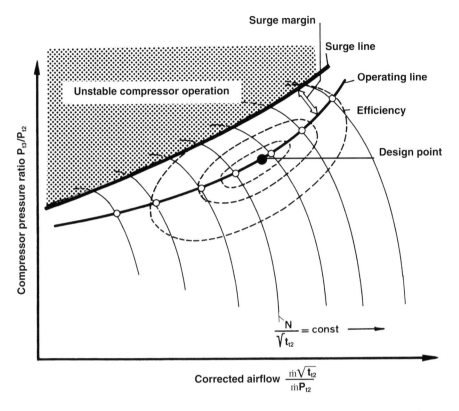

Fig 4-18   Compressor map showing compressor pressure ratio versus mass flow rate

adopted throughout the propulsion community as a standard. Among those of greatest importance are the following two parameters:

*   the Corrected Mass Flow Rate at the compressor face (station 2) is defined as

$$\frac{\dot{m}\sqrt{t_{t2}}}{p_{t2}}$$

*   the Corrected Engine Speed defined as $\dfrac{N}{\sqrt{t_{t2}}}$

Using corrected parameters, a compressor map is universally applicable, independent of meteorological conditions of the testing day. Frequently, data is referenced to the compressor design point, allowing lines of constant corrected wheel speed and corrected mass flow rate to be given as percentages of design conditions.

Finally, the *operating line*. It will be remembered that a speed curve was obtained by changing the exit area of the compressor exhaust duct. The majority of jet engines, however, utilize a constant-area (non-adjustable) nozzle. In this case, only one point is possible on each speed curve. Connecting these points yields the *operating line* of the particular engine (**Fig 4-18**).

Engines with afterburning are employed to power combat aircraft and the Concorde supersonic airliner. Such engines feature one operating line for each nozzle setting.

4.5   Compressor operation

Basically there are two modes of compressor work that have to be considered: *stationary* mode where engine parameters do not change (cruising flight), and *transient* mode where engine parameters rapidly change (engine accelerating to maximum thrust).

Steady-state operation is depicted by the equilibrium operating line which denotes balance of power between compressor and turbine, i.e. the turbine provides just as much power as the compressor (including auxiliaries) demands. Aircraft flight operations require the engine to be able to intercept any point of the operating line quickly. During these transients, deviation from the steady-state operating line is permitted for short periods. Hazardous flow conditions, however, are not allowed to occur.

In this respect the most critical phase is when the engine is accelerated. Accelerating the compressor can be accomplished only by having the turbine produce more power than the compressor is able to absorb. This happens by the injecting and burning of additional fuel, much like opening the throttle in a car engine. As a result, turbine inlet temperature t_{t4} will rise, which has the effect that engine components downstream of the compressor (combustor, turbine, nozzle) are momentarily less accepting of the flow (throttle effect). This in turn causes compressor discharge pressure (upstream) to rise, and the compressor pressure ratio to rise, too. This condition could be hazardous to the compressor if the power transient were to cause the compressor to exceed the surge line. In order to minimize the risk of the compressor surging, a *surge margin* (between operating line and surge line) is provided, usually by setting maximum operating line pressure ratios 20 per cent below those of the surge line.

A large surge margin is, however, generally impossible to maintain over the entire operating regime of the compressor. At low corrected engine speeds, for example, if no corrective action is taken at the compressor, the steady-state operating line will unavoidably approach the surge line, with a risk of blade vibration (the origin of which will be dealt with subsequently).

As a precaution, compressors employ either of two methods:

a)   bleeding air at a mid-compressor stage in order to adjust mass flow rate to the turbine's demand;

b)   modulating compressor airflow by variable stator vanes. Examples will be given in the subsequent section.

A lapse in the operating line, that is where the operating line is approaching the surge line, indicates where unsteady compressor operation may be hazardous. This may happen either at very low or at very high corrected compressor speeds, indicated by either too low or too high total temperature values t_{t2} at the compressor face. The key to avoiding a hazardous situation is by knowing under which conditions these temperatures occur. It will be recalled that total temperature t_t is formed by static temperature t plus a quantity containing Mach number (Chapter 2). Therefore, high total temperatures occur when flying at high speed (M large) and low level (t large), whereas low total temperatures result from flying low-speed at high altitudes (because temperature decreases with altitude). From this it can easily be deduced that combat aircraft flying high-speed low-level sorties may face compressor problems, whereas passenger transport aircraft always fly slowly in the vicinity of the ground because they are either landing or taking off. At high altitudes, however, any aircraft must avoid flying slowly (because of low Mach number and low temperature). This could, for example, inadvertently happen to a passenger aircraft flying a holding pattern at altitude. As a precaution, the engine manufacturer will clearly state what the safe operational limits of his engines are.

Consider now the case of an (inadvertent) engine operation beyond the surge limit. A distinction must first be made between two modes of unsteady compressor operation, *surge* and *rotating stall*.

Surge may be explained as a mismatch of the compressor on the one hand, and downstream engine components on the other (combustor, turbine, nozzle). These downstream components may be considered to function as a single unit, with a characteristic that can also be drawn on the compressor map (**Fig 4-19**).

Now consider the compressor to operate on the safe side of, but close to, the surge line (point B). If for some reason airflow rate is reduced, the pressure ratio of the combustor–turbine–nozzle system will decrease (point 1), but the pressure ratio of the compressor will decrease even more (point 2). The result is a relieving of the high pressure in the compressor due to pressure equalizing in the upstream direction, causing the combustor–turbine–nozzle system to become

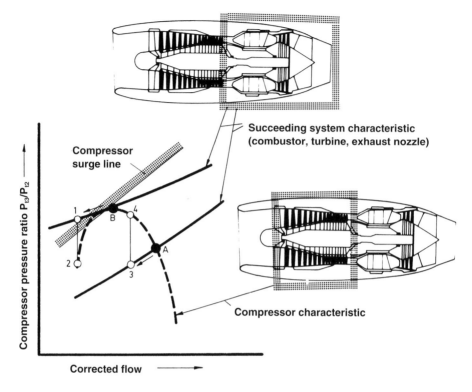

Fig 4-19 Explaining compressor surge

less restrictive to the airflow, and compressor airflow to recover (compressor operating returning to point B). This surging action may occur several hundred times per second, causing audible engine buzz and severe engine vibration. Consequences to the engine may range from simple decay of thrust to total engine destruction.

Now consider that the compressor is operating at point A, a safe distance away from the surge line. A reduction of airflow will again cause a reduction of the pressure ratio within the combustor–turbine–nozzle system (point 3), but the compressor, even at this reduced airflow, is able to deliver a higher pressure ratio (point 4). In this case pressure equalization is accomplished without causing a hazard to the engine (return to point A).

So much for the engine surge. However, there exists another mode of unstable compressor operation which can initiate blade vibration, and be rapidly succeeded by blade failure. To explain this phenomenon, we start with the assumption that the compressor is working at the border of, but still within, its safe operating envelope, and at low rotating speed. In this case the forward stages will operate closer to the surge boundary than the middle or end stages. A small local perturbation may be sufficient to trigger flow separation on just one blade (**Fig 4-20**). Such local flow separation will reduce the mass flow rate within the flow passage between two neighbouring blades as it acts like a local blockage. As a consequence, flow velocity upstream of the blade concerned will decrease, causing the approaching flow to deviate away from the fluid obstacle. This will mean that the flow angle-of-attack at the first blade will decrease (1) and that of a succeeding blade increase (2). As the flow at the first blade recovers, flow of the succeeding blade will separate. A third blade is about to encounter this perturbation zone (3).

The separation sequence appears to move opposite to the direction of rotation and successively befalls each approaching blade, though only for a fraction of a second. This mode of unstable compressor operation is termed *rotating stall*. Investigations have shown the circumferential stall propagation velocity to be slower than the rotating speed of the blades.

Rotating stall may not be confined to a single blade cell as shown, but may spread over two or more neighbouring cells. Because of the

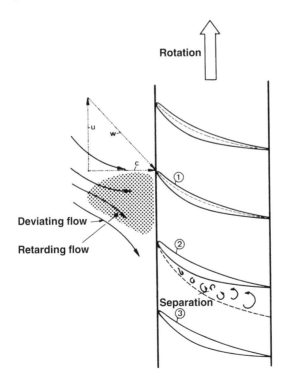

Fig 4-20   Explaining rotating stall

unsteady character, blade vibration is likely to occur that may end up in blade failure.

Over the years, engine designers have developed methods that have greatly reduced the risk of rotating stall.

4.6 Compressor case studies

Having learned about flow phenomena that can occur in a single compressor stage, we will now turn to some typical hardware examples among the variety of compressor designs. In doing so, it will be useful to consider the compressor not as an isolated component, but rather in the context of the complete jet engine.

The multi-stage axial compressor was evolved because the pressure increase required for higher power outputs could not be provided by a single stage. It was found, however, that aerodynamic loading is not distributed evenly within a compressor assembly, a factor that has to be taken into account when designing an efficient engine.

Arriving at a good design appears to be least difficult for the design point, since well-defined requirements in terms of mass flow rate, pressure ratio and rotation speed must be met. Additionally, however, acceptable compressor operation is also required at off-design con-

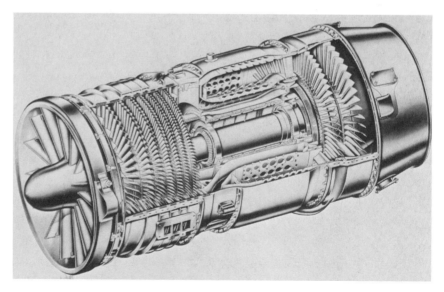

Fig 4-21   Single-spool turbojet with low compression ratio (General Electric CJ-610, 8-stage compressor, compressor pressure ratio $p_{t3}/p_{t2} = 6.8$, mass flow rate 20 kg/s, rotational speed 16,500 rpm, static thrust 12.65 kN/2800 lb)

ditions, thus calling for stable engine operation over a large operating envelope. This has led to compressor construction developing along quasi-standard lines.

Turbojet engines
In its simplest form, this type engine is confined to the low-thrust class spectrum of smaller jet-propelled aircraft. Because of a relatively small number of compressor stages, operation is straightforward requiring little or no sophisticated means of adjusting the flow within the compressor. Typical is a single-spool assembly of turbine and compressor. The plain turbojet, although reliable in operation, has a low position on the ladder of efficiency, and, moreover, is extremely noisy. Which is why it is today to be found only in the older civil aircraft that were not hushkitted, or in some military jets.

To raise the efficiency of a plain turbojet requires considerable effort, in particular with regard to off-design characteristics. At off-design conditions, the front stages are more highly loaded than the middle or rear stages, causing the front stages to operate closer to the surge boundary, whereas the middle and rear stages operate at a safe margin (**Fig 4-17**). By adjusting the flow with variable stator

Fig 4-22   Variable stators on inlet guide vanes and forward stator rows to relieve compressor front stages from high aerodynamic loading at off-design conditions. Blade adjustment is accomplished by hydraulic jack, angle lever and actuating ring (General Electric J-79 turbojet engine)

vanes in the front stages, the optimum angle-of-attack is provided for the rotor blades that is necessary for engine off-design airflow demand.

The design concept of variable stator vanes was pioneered by General Electric, who also successfully employed this method with smaller engines and even turboshafts. The concept has demonstrated that high performance is possible even with single-spool engines as shown by the famous J79 engine of the late fifties, once powering a number of the most modern airplane types of their day, such as F-104, F-4, B-58, and Vigilante.

Turbofan engines
The low propulsive efficiency of the pure turbojet engine at the medium to high subsonic speeds at which civil transports operate, led to the development of engine design featuring an additional, secondary air passage surrounding the primary or core engine. The secondary airstream essentially has its own engine cycle featuring a separate compression and expansion process. This type of engine is termed a *bypass* or *turbofan* engine. The mechanical energy to compress the airstream is supplied by the primary or core engine and transferred through either a single- or multi-stage fan.

A once innovative solution of the turbofan principle, the aft-fan, was developed by General Electric in the sixties. Turbine and fan form one unit which can rotate freely and independently, as no mechanical connection to the core engine exists. Connection is purely aerodynam-

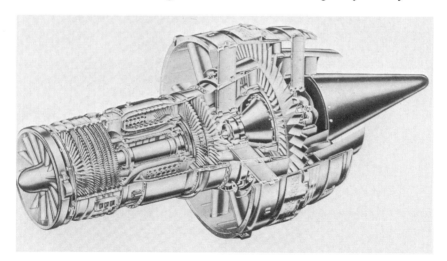

Fig 4-23   Developed from the millitary J85 turbojet engine, this early civil turbofan resulted by adding a single-stage turbine/fan unit to the rear of the original turbojet (General Electric CF–700)

ical, through the gas stream of the core engine. This method, at a time when the turbofan engine was in its infancy, constituted a relatively simple way to develop a turbofan engine from an existing turbojet. The very same principle was also applied when deriving from the military J79 turbojet the civil C-805 turbofan engine that was used to power the Convair Coronado four-engined transport.

A major disadvantage of this design is the greatly differing temperatures in the single turbine/fan wheel assembly which materials of this compact design must sustain: high temperatures at the inner turbine blades, low temperatures at the outer fan blades. Because of these difficulties, the aft-fan type was eventually abandoned, to give way to the front-fan type, nowadays the only type existing.

After passing through a common air intake and the front fan, the low-compressed airstream then divides to the outer (cold) bypass flow and the inner (hot) core engine flow. While the inner airstream is entering the gas generator section of the engine (where it will be further compressed, heated and expanded), the fan airstream is passing through a duct, at the discharge end of which it accelerates through an exhaust nozzle without receiving any more energy.

Another milestone in the development of the modern turbine engine resulted from the fact that a high-performance multi-stage compressor is difficult to control because all the rotor blades are operating at the same rotational speed. This led to the two-spool compressor arrangement, where the compression process is shared by two smaller, separate compressor units, each of which has about half the number of stages

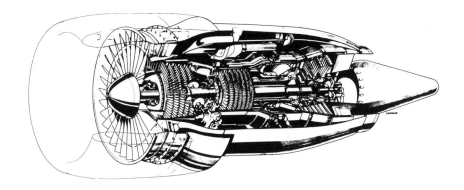

Fig 4-24   Turbofan engine Rolls-Royce M45H featuring a front fan

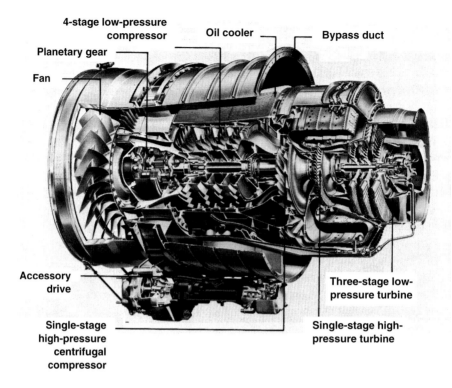

Fig 4-25   Turbofan engine featuring axial and radial compressor layout (Garrett AlResearch TFE 731-2, 16.8 kN thrust, compressor pressure ratio $p_{t3}/p_{t2} = 14.6$)

of the single-spool unit. Each compressor is driven by its own separate turbine and both halves can thereby operate at different rotational speeds. Because there are no mechanical links between the compressors, operation is very flexible as either unit can be adjusted to run at optimum speed. Reflecting their function, the first compressor is termed the *low-pressure compressor* (LPC), the rear compressor the *high-pressure compressor* (HPC).

An interesting development of a multi-stage two-spool compressor was developed by Garrett with the TFE731 engine (**Fig 4-25**). A three-stage low-pressure turbine drives a four-stage low-pressure compressor and also, via a reduction gear, a single-stage fan. A single-stage high-pressure compressor of radial type is driven by a single-stage high-pressure turbine – a noteworthy combination of axial and radial compressors in a very compact arrangement.

High bypass-ratio turbofans

An important parameter in classifying a turbofan engine is bypass-ratio (BPR), which denotes the amount of air *bypassing* the core engine relative to the airflow going *through* the core engine. The range of bypass-ratio today is between 0.2 and 8. High bypass-ratio engines are classified as having a bypass-ratio of over 5.

High bypass-ratio engines with more than 50,000 lb (222 kN) of thrust are used to power modern widebody transport aircraft. These engines, developed from first-generation turbofans, are remarkable because of the tremendous power they are able to generate – evidenced by their size.

It may be worthwhile to recall the underlying principle of this large amount of thrust by referring to the thrust definition of Chapter 2:

Thrust = air mass flow rate × velocity change

$$T \quad = \dot{m} \text{ (kg/s)} \quad \times (V_9 - V_0) \text{ (m/s)}$$

According to this definition, a high thrust figure is achieved either

Fig 4-26   The large-diameter fan is the characteristic feature of high-bypass ratio turbofan engines (Pratt & Whitney JT-9D)

by a high exit velocity V_9 of the exhausting gas, or by a large air mass flow rate ṁ exhausting at a moderate exit velocity V_9. It was the latter choice which led to the development of the high bypass-ratio turbofan, whose typical feature is a fan diameter of over 2.5 metres (100 inch).

Particularly noteworthy are long fan blades that enable air mass flow rates of over 600 kilograms per second being processed. The power transmitted within the compact space of the fan requires a characteristic fan construction, which will be detailed next by referring to the CF6 high bypass-ratio turbofan of General Electric.

The CF6-6 series fan assembly comprises a single-stage fan (long blades) and an additional booster stage downstream (short blades, **Fig 4-27**). The booster stage, basically a low-pressure compressor, is required to further compress that part of the airflow (about 16 per cent) which enters the core engine. Later series of the CF6 engine, e.g. the CF6-50A, feature a three-stage booster. Downstream of the low-pressure compressor (booster), variable bypass valves are provided to discharge air into the fan stream to establish proper flow-matching between the low and high pressure spools during transient operation. Engine testing of the fan/low-pressure compressor unit with its automatic control and bleed system has shown excellent stall margin characteristics. As has become usual in the design of modern large fans,

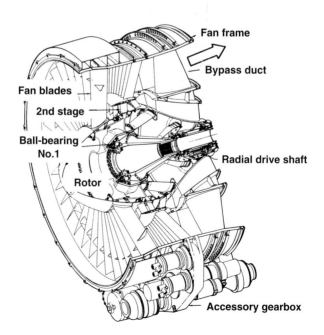

Fig 4-27   Fan section of a high bypass-ratio engine (General Electric CF6-6)

Fig 4-28   Typical circular-arc airfoil shape of fan blade upper section operating at supersonic velocity. To reduce weight, each blade has 22 holes. Behind fan is a three-stage booster to raise pressure of core engine flow (General Electric CF6-6)

there are no inlet guide vanes. Canted outlet guide vanes are used to reduce swirl velocity of fan air downstream of the rotor to keep noise levels low (see Chapter 10).

The CF6 fan has 38 titanium fan blades, each carrying 22 drilled holes at the tip, both to reduce weight and to keep resonance frequencies outside the engine operating range. Because the tip of a fan blade is operating at supersonic velocity, the aerofoil section at the tip is of circular arc type in conformity with the characteristics of supersonic flow, while classical (subsonic) wing sections are found in the lower part of the same blade as this part is operating at subsonic speeds.

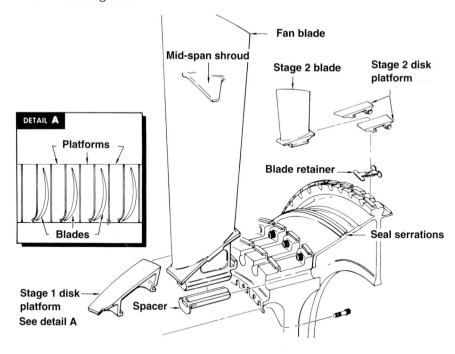

Fig 4-29   Fan blade assembly to rotor disk (General Electric CF6-6)

In order to minimize the aerodynamic drag of the installed engine, it is necessary to make the overall diameter as small as possible. In the case of the CF6 engine, this resulted in the use of a small hub radius and, therefore, low wheel speed at the blade root. In order to maintain the required efficiency and stall margin figures, it was necessary for the fan blade to be designed as a non-constant energy stage; that is to say more energy is transmitted at the tip than at the hub. The low-pressure compressor must therefore supply additional energy which is required to provide a constant radial pressure ratio (over the blade from root to tip) at the exit of the low-pressure compressor.

Length of the fan blades makes blade vibration control and the avoidance of high vibratory stress a key consideration in the fan mechanical design, in order to ensure a 30,000-hour life. One of the structural elements that reduce blade vibration are mid-span shrouds that lean to neighbouring shrouds to form a damping ring structure. Other factors that would degrade service life such as foreign object damage, blade erosion due to rain, hailstone and ice ingestion, and high inlet distortion, had also to be taken into account early in the design.

The aeroelastic design permitted the fan to sustain loads at 120 per cent overspeed, as required by the FAA. To withstand such excessive

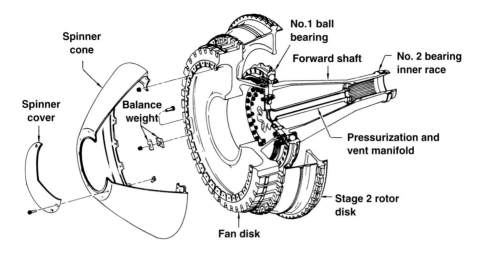

Spinner cone

Spinner cover

Balance weight

No.1 ball bearing

Forward shaft

No. 2 bearing inner race

Pressurization and vent manifold

Stage 2 rotor disk

Fan disk

Fig 4-30   Fan rotor layout (General Electric CF6-6)

loads, blades are made of forged titanium which provides ample strength at minimum weight.

A crucial area in the design of a fan is where the blades join the rotor disk. Because of the high loads that have to be transmitted, a close and reliable matching of both components is of paramount importance. Added to this is the requirement that individual blades can be removed from the rotor with the engine installed in the aircraft. These requirements are well met by designing the fan blade root as a 'dovetail' that fits into a matching slot of the rotor disk (**Fig 4-29**). The basic dovetail shape used in the CF6 engine has proven reliable in a number of General Electric turbofan and turbojet engine designs.

The *rotor disk* must accept all loads from the blades and transmit forces to the engine structure. In order to provide a reliable disk, titanium was chosen because of its optimum strength-to-weight ratio commensurate with the requirements of greatest safety in airline service.

Loads that have to be sustained by the rotor disk are:

– centrifugal forces due to rotation

– axial and bending forces due to aerodynamic loads of the blades

– vibratory stress

Two bearings support the fan rotor assembly. The forward bearing is a thrust bearing, the rear bearing a roller bearing (**Fig 4-30**). Rotor shaft, disk and spacers are attached by fitted dowel bolts.

Usually, a large number of tests is required to ensure that the fan construction is capable of withstanding all loads that occur in daily service, without impairing the life requirement of many thousands of hours (30,000 hours and more in the case of the CF6-6). Some of the tests also require the ingestion of birds, which the blades must withstand.

5 Combustion chamber

The necessity for fuel to be burnt at the highest level of efficiency is fundamental in the aero gas turbine engine. Combustion efficiency directly affects the fuel load/aircraft weight/payload equation, and therefore the operating costs and range performance. Added to this are environmental problems calling for a reduction of dangerous emissions that result from combustion.

The development of combustion chambers is based essentially on experience with previous systems of similar design. In spite of a multitude of possible solutions for a particular combustion system, certain principles of design will be found in any combustion chamber.

5.1   The combustion process

The basic task of the combustion chamber is to provide a stream of hot gas that is able to release its energy to the turbine and nozzle sections of the engine. Following an increase in pressure through the compressor section, heat is added to the airflow by the burning of a combustible gaseous mixture of vaporized fuel and highly-compressed air. The combustion process is confined within the constrained volume of the combustion chamber and must be accomplished at a minimal loss of pressure (constant-pressure combustion).

Combustion chamber refinement was greatly influenced by requirements resulting from the increase in air traffic and the environmental pollution that came with it (see Chapter 10). Before going into the details of combustion chamber layout, let us look at what happens within a combustion chamber; in this case one of the can type used in early engines (**Fig 5-1**).

The air mass flow when discharged from the compressor enters the combustion chamber at a velocity of around 150 m/s (490 ft/sec) – far too high to sustain a flame for combustion. What is required in the first place is a slowing down of the airflow. This is achieved in the forward section of the combustion chamber which is formed as a diffuser; that is, the flow passage cross-section increases in the downstream direction. The result not only is a decrease in airflow velocity, but at the same time a further increase in pressure. Airflow velocity is now around 25 m/s (80 ft/s), still too high for orderly burning of the kerosine/air mixture. Flow velocity, therefore, must be further diminished

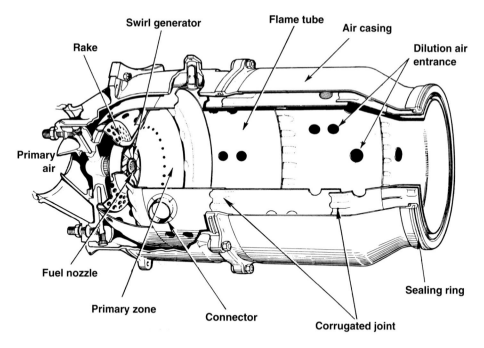

Fig 5-1　Typical can-type burner assembly

down to a few metres per second. This is accomplished by means of a perforated disk that surrounds the fuel nozzle.

The second essential task of the combustion chamber is to provide the correct fuel/air mixture. The mass ratio of the two components that react in the combustion process, namely fuel mass injected per second and air mass forced each second into the combustion chamber, varies with the operating conditions of the aircraft and may range between ratios of 1:45 to 1:130. The fuel/air ratio for efficient combustion, however, is in the order of 1:15, which means that only a fraction of the incoming air is required for the combustion process. The task of reducing flow velocity for the orderly burning of the fuel and apportioning the airflow to achieve complete combustion, is accomplished in the forward section of the combustion chamber.

Apportioning the air for combustion is achieved by means of a short air duct (snout), which has a number of drag-producing swirl vanes at its exit to reduce flow velocity. Airflow passing through the snout is only 20 per cent of the total mass of air entering the combustion chamber. By far the largest part is ducted around the internal flame tube, from where gradual admixing within the flame tube is made by

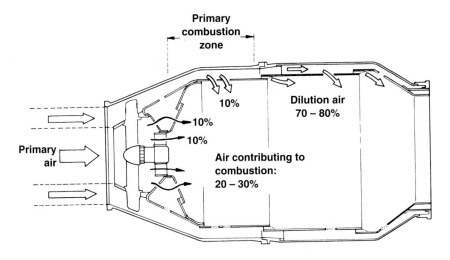

Fig 5-2   Schematic flow in combustion chamber

means of various-size holes arranged behind the primary combustion zone (**Fig 5-2**).

Fuel is pumped into the injection nozzle at high pressure. The form of the injection nozzle ensures that the vaporized fuel is discharged as a spray cone which provides intensive mixing with the air passing by (Chapter 9). Fuel burning takes place in a relatively small space within the flame tube, the *primary combustion zone*, where temperatures may be as high as 2,000K (3,600R). No flame tube material would be able to withstand such temperatures if the walls were not intensively cooled. To this end a system of small holes and slots in the liner wall allows secondary cooling air to provide a protective shield in order to insulate the flametube walls from the super-hot flames (**Fig 5-3**). The remaining part of the secondary air (about 50 per cent) is ducted along the flame tube and gradually added to the hot gas. The combustion process must have ended before this to prevent incomplete combustion due to 'low' temperatures.

Combustion is usually initiated by electrical spark ignition and then continues as a self-sustaining process.

5.2   Combustion chamber characteristics

The requirements for optimum combustion must be met at certain critical aircraft operating conditions, e.g. flight speed, cruising flight at

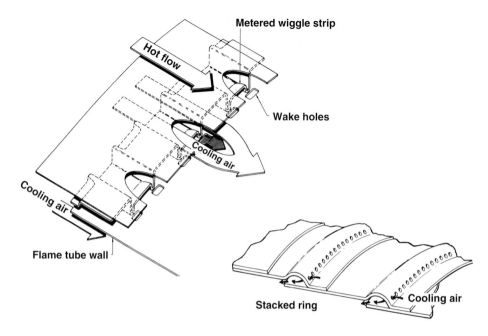

Fig 5-3   Cooling of combustion chamber liner (General Electric CF6)

altitude, accelerating during take-off etc. Specific parameters are used to describe combustion chamber characteristics.

Efficiency of combustion
In general, the injected fuel does not burn completely and thus produces less heat than would be possible theoretically. The reason is that apportioning the exact amount of air necessary for complete combustion is difficult to achieve, and particularly with respect to the wide range of aircraft operating conditions.

The degree of actual fuel usage is characterized by a combustion efficiency factor giving the amount of heat released by combustion in relation to the heat theoretically available in the fuel:

$$\text{combustion efficiency} = \frac{\text{heat released}, Q}{\text{heat theoret. available}, Q_0}$$

Modern combustion chambers achieve efficiencies between 90 to 98 per cent ($\eta_c = 0.90$–0.98). Values could be much improved if stoichiometric combustion were possible, i.e. if the correct amount of air completely to burn a given amount of fuel were apportioned. This is not yet achievable.

Another important performance parameter is *total pressure loss*, because in a gas turbine cycle the aim is to attain combustion at constant pressure. Some loss of pressure will unavoidably be incurred due to the swirl necessary for efficient combustion, and due to friction. These losses have to be minimized by careful design of the combustion chamber. The amount of total pressure loss is characterized by the ratio of total pressures at combustion chamber discharge, p_{t4}, and total pressure at combustion chamber entrance, p_{t3}.

Total pressure loss $\Pi_c = \dfrac{p_{t4}}{p_{t3}}$

Typical values of the total pressure loss coefficient are between 0.93 and 0.98, which means pressure losses are between 2 and 7 per cent.

Stable operating range
In contrast to a ground-based gas turbine plant, a turbo-propulsive engine used for aircraft is subject to large variations of engine speed and operating altitude. Within the complete operating envelope ranging from flight idle thrust to max take-off thrust, and from sea level static pressure to low pressure at altitude, extinction of the flame in the combustion chamber must be prevented.

According to varying operating conditions the following quantities change at combustion chamber entry:

– static pressure, p_3

– static temperature, t_3

– airflow velocity

The stable operating range is usually characterized by a permissible margin of the fuel/air ratio at which stable combustion is maintained. The operating range is narrowed by decreasing atmospheric pressure with increase of flight altitude, which will cause entry pressure into the combustion chamber to diminish (**Fig 5-4**). Jet engines feature a high pressure ratio (such as the modern high bypass-ratio engines used in subsonic transports) are less sensitive to this effect. In the case of a stoichiometric fuel/air ratio stable combustion would be maintained even at less favourable conditions.

The combustion process is also sensitive to a high entry velocity into the combustion chamber which may cause the flame to be carried away.

Temperature distribution
Optimum engine performance will be achieved if the average temperature of the hot gas is as close as possible to the temperature tolerable

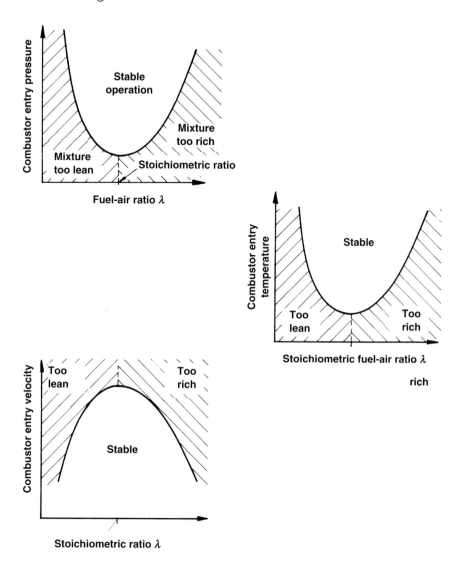

Fig 5-4   Factors affecting flame stability

to the turbine blades. If the temperature distribution is non-uniform such that hot spots exist in the gas, the turbine entry temperature must be reduced to prevent damage to the blades. This will inevitably reduce engine performance.

A more intense mixing of the fuel with the airflow generally improves temperature distribution, but may increase total pressure loss (= flow losses) in the combustion chamber.

Starting
Ignition of the fuel/air mixture is made easier if pressure and temperature is high and flow velocity is low. If the fuel/air mixture is too lean or too rich, ignition will be impaired.

Deposits
In case of a rich fuel/air mixture, the tendency of molecular carbon to form deposits is increased because the available oxygen is insufficient for complete combustion. Changing the fuel/air ratio may also change the location in the combustion chamber where carbon will be deposited.

Deposits are also dependent on fuel quality which may greatly vary between airports.

The several reasons given above illustrate that combustion chamber design requires careful assessment of contradictory factors.

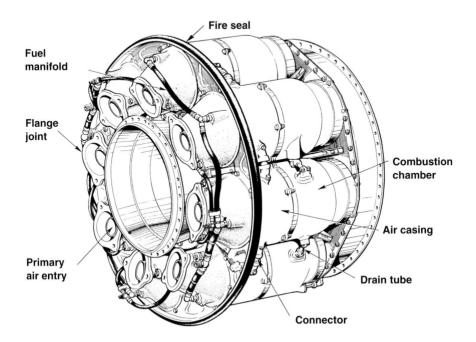

Fig 5-5   Circumferentially arranged can-type burners

5.3   Types of combustors

Classification of combustion chamber types is made according to geometrical characteristics. There are basically three types:

- can-type burners

- annular-type burners

- can-annular type burners

5.3.1   Can-type combustion chamber

This type is found in early jet engines. A number of single burners are arranged in parallel circumferentially around the engine axis. Each chamber is supplied with a stream of airflow by a separate air duct that connects upstream to the compressor outlet (**Fig 5-5**). Burners are linked by interconnectors that enable the flame to spread to neighbouring combustors, thus igniting the fuel/air mixture there, whereas start-up ignition is made only at two combustors. The interconnectors also act in equalizing the pressure among all burner cans to ensure iden-

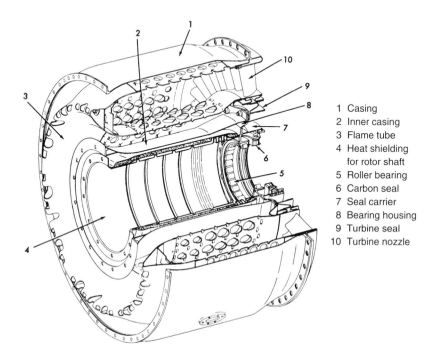

1 Casing
2 Inner casing
3 Flame tube
4 Heat shielding
  for rotor shaft
5 Roller bearing
6 Carbon seal
7 Seal carrier
8 Bearing housing
9 Turbine seal
10 Turbine nozzle

Fig 5-6   Annular-type combustion chamber (General Electric CJ610)

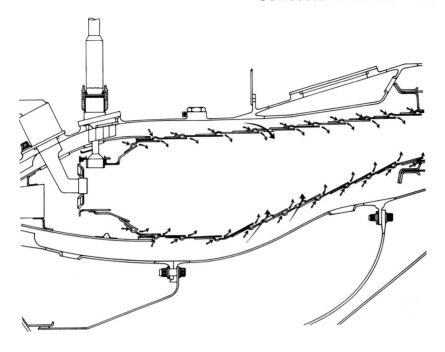

Fig 5-7   Schematic flow in annular combustion chamber (General Electric CF6)

tical operating conditions in all combustors and thereby prevent asymmetric turbine loading.

Because of the inefficient use of available space and inherently unfavourable fluid dynamic effects, the can-type burner is no longer used in aero-engines. However, it did constitute a necessary step in turbo-engine development.

5.3.2 Annular-type combustion chamber
The annular-type combustor provides the most efficient use of volumetric space. Basically, the annular-type burner is a single concentric flame tube surrounding the spools (**Fig 5-6**). A major benefit of this type of burner is a 25 per cent reduction in weight, as compared to the can-type burner. In addition, circumferential pressure equalizing is greatly enhanced. Being a single large combustion chamber, the process of combustion is more evenly achieved within the flame tube.

5.3.3 Can-annular-type combustors
An intermediate solution towards the modern annular-type combustor was the can-annular-type. For engines developed in the sixties, military and civil alike, the can-annular burner was the prevailing type.

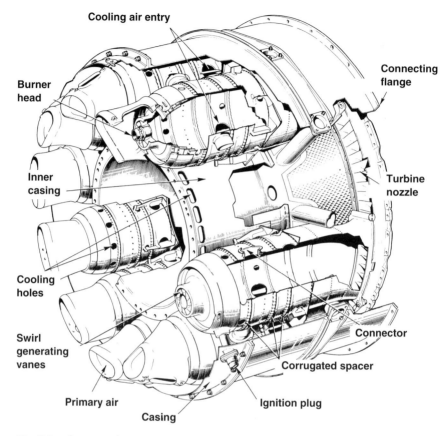

Cooling air entry

Connecting flange

Burner head

Inner casing

Turbine nozzle

Cooling holes

Swirl generating vanes

Connector

Corrugated spacer

Primary air

Ignition plug

Casing

Fig 5-8   Can-annular-type combustion chamber

The supply of secondary air to the flame tubes is made through a common air casing while primary air for combustion is supplied through individual air intakes (**Fig 5-8**). The flame tubes are mounted to a circular rim-like arrangement of the turbine nozzles where the flow expands and accelerates.

A special solution of the can-annular-type burner was developed by Pratt & Whitney which featured six fuel injection nozzles mounted in circular clusters within each flame tube. The design resembles a miniature annular combustor and eight were used in the JT4 engine.

In its time, the can-annular-type burner represented economical use of available space and provided good mechanical stability of the overall construction.

Fig 5-9 Can-annular-type combustion chamber (General Electric J79)

Fig 5-10 Cutaway through burner with six fuel nozzles (Pratt & Whitney JT4)

6 Turbine

The primary task of the turbine in an aero-engine is to drive the compressor. Additionally the turbine must drive the accessories. In the case of a turboprop engine the primary task of the turbine is to drive the propellers, and in the case of a shaft engine to drive the rotor blades of a helicopter.

The tremendous turbine power which may attain values of more than 50,000 hp, is accomplished by extracting part, or practically all, of the energy contained in the hot gas. A single turbine blade alone may contribute as much as 250 hp – more than many large car engines are capable of producing.

The progress made in turbine engine technology becomes more apparent if one considers that the energy conversion is accomplished in the limited volume of a turbine, and at extremely high temperature loadings. The advance to large engines producing more than 20 tons of thrust became possible only after new materials and improved cooling methods became available.

6.1   Turbine design and operation

Basically turbine operation is no different from that of a compressor. Whilst a compressor is adding energy to the airflow passing through it by converting mechanical energy into pressure energy, a turbine conversely absorbs energy from the gas flow to convert it into mechanical shaft power or torque.

In aero engines, the axial-type turbine is exclusively used because of the higher mass flow rate it makes possible. A radial-type turbine is, in fact, also possible, but is not a practical alternative. Design of the axial flow turbine can be single- or multi-stage. A turbine stage comprises two main elements consisting of:

a)   a set of stationary nozzle guide vanes followed downstream by
b)   a set of rotating blades. (In a compressor this sequence is reversed, *cf* Chapter 4.)

The stator is formed as a ring of stationary radial vanes inside the turbine casing, the vanes being of aerofoil section with their leading edges facing the flow coming from the combustion section. In the

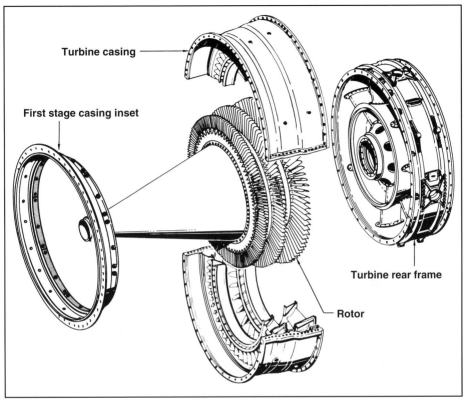

Fig 6-1   Assembly of a high-performance turbine (General Electric J79)

narrowing flow path between adjacent blades, the hot gas is accelerated to high velocity. Because of this nozzle effect the stationary vanes
are termed *nozzle guide vanes*, and their complete arrangement constitutes the *turbine nozzle*. The rotating wheel that follows the turbine
nozzle downstream is the actual turbine (**Fig 6-1**).
   Factors affecting the number of turbine stages are:

   – the number of compressor spools

   – the amount of energy that must be extracted from the hot gas

   – the rotational velocity (rpm)

   – the maximum permissible turbine diameter

   High compression ratios typical of modern engines require multi-
stage turbines.
   The question may be asked how it is that a gas expands in a turbine
and compresses in a compressor. The answer lies in blade design. In the

Chapter on compressors we saw that the flow cross-section between adjacent blades is designed to increase in the downstream direction, and we call this a diffuser. The effect of a diffuser is to decelerate the flow and convert its kinetic energy into pressure energy.

In a turbine the condition is reversed. Because the flow cross-section between adjacent blades narrows in the downstream direction, a nozzle effect exists which causes the flow to accelerate and make it ready to perform work.

As the gas expands, its pressure and temperature decrease while velocity rapidly increases. A turbine stage is classified according to the amount of energy converted in the stator and the rotor sections, respectively. A distinction is made between:

- the constant-pressure turbine,
- the impulse turbine,
- and a mixture of both.

Aero-engines feature the mixed turbine type. Before considering these, let us first attend to the function of the nozzle guide vanes.

6.1.1   Turbine nozzle

In order to perform work, the hot gas discharged from the combustion chamber must be suitably processed. This is the task of nozzle guide vanes, and they have two principal functions. First, they must convert part of the energy of the hot gas into kinetic energy in order to make the flow fast enough when it impinges on the rotor blades. Second, the nozzle guide vanes must change the direction of the gas flow in a manner such that the circumferential forces engendered in the blades are maximized for the production of shaft power.

The required acceleration is accomplished by narrowing the passage between adjacent blades (nozzle effect). As velocity increases, static pressure and temperature decrease. The degree of this energy conversion depends on the relationship of nozzle inlet to exit area which is a direct function of the type of turbine blades used.

In high-performance jet engines the nozzle guide vanes are designed to obtain 'critical' pressure at nozzle exit, i.e. an inlet-to-exit area ratio is selected which provides speed of sound gas velocity at the nozzle exit.

As no work is done by the hot gas in the nozzle guide vane section (because they are stationary), the gas total energy will remain constant, if flow losses are neglected. It is only the state of part of the energy that is changing from the potential to the kinetic, i.e. heat and pressure energy are converted into gas velocity energy.

Important to the design of nozzle guide vanes is a careful selection of the inlet cross-section. If the area is too small, aerodynamic drag will rise causing an increase of back pressure at the compressor discharge. This will bring the compressor operating line closer to the surge line, which can cause problems during engine acceleration. Conversely, if the nozzle guide vanes feature a large inlet cross-section, engine acceleration characteristics will improve, but a higher specific fuel consumption will be incurred. The final decision will be a compromise of these criteria.

6.1.2   Constant-pressure turbine

A characteristic of the *impulse* or *constant-pressure turbine*, and the nozzle guide vanes it uses, is that gas expansion occurs only in the nozzle guide vane section of the stage because it is here that gas potential energy is converted to kinetic energy.

The gas when exiting from the nozzle guide vanes at high velocity, will impinge on the rotor blades. The consequent wheel rotation is accomplished through momentum exchange from turning the gas flow path by the rotor blades, at constant pressure. Ensuring that pressure remains constant is achieved by keeping the flow path cross-section constant between adjacent rotor blades.

The impulse turbine is essentially the same as the well-known water wheel. Its principle of operation will be explained by using a turbine cascade formed by supposedly unwrapping the rotor wheel onto a plane.

The gas flow enters the nozzle guide vanes at absolute velocity C_0, and exits at much higher absolute velocity C_1, in a direction imposed by the geometry of the vanes (**Fig 6-2a**). Due to wheel rotation at constant circumferential velocity u_1, each rotating blade 'views' the gas as approaching from a different direction and at a different (relative) velocity w_1. All three velocity vectors (c, u, w) may be combined to form a velocity triangle at rotor wheel entry. As the gas passes through the rotor flow path, it changes direction, but the value of the relative velocity remains constant ($w_2 = w_1$). Because circumferential velocity u_2 at the rotor exit, due to wheel geometry, is the same as at rotor entry ($u_1 = u_2$), the velocity triangle at rotor wheel exit is completely resolved.

Note that absolute velocity C_2 (and hence kinetic energy $\frac{C_2^2}{2}$) is lower than at rotor wheel entry, due to the work transmitted from the gas to the rotor blades.

The character of the impulse turbine is illustrated by its gas characteristics across a turbine stage (**Fig 6-2a**, left). As a result of the gas expanding in the nozzle guide vanes, pressure and temperature will decrease while velocity increases. The drop in absolute velocity c in the rotor section of the stage results directly from the energy transmitted from gas to blades. While static pressure remains constant, temperature rises due to friction.

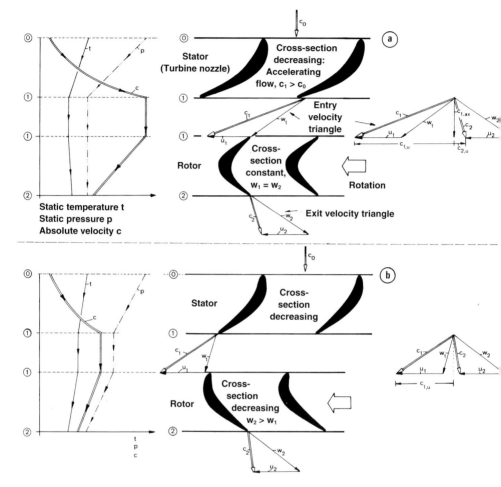

Fig 6-2 Turbine stage
  a) constant-pressure turbine
  b) reaction turbine

6.1.3   Reaction turbine

The characteristic of the reaction turbine is that expansion of the gas takes place not only in the nozzle guide vane section, but also through the rotating blades of the rotor wheel. When passing the nozzle guide vanes, the hot gas is accelerated while temperature and pressure decrease, much like the impulse turbine but to a lesser degree (**Fig 6-2b**). Since rotor blades also feature narrowing cross-sections of the flow path between adjacent blades, a nozzle effect exists which causes the flow to accelerate further. Analogous to the lifting force of a wing, an aerodynamic force is generated on the rotor blades which rotates the wheel. This, however, is not the only power source that rotates a reaction turbine. A certain amount of momentum action exists, generated when the accelerated gas impinges on the rotor blades. A benefit of the reaction turbine is better efficiency than the impulse turbine, whereas the impulse turbine makes possible the higher power output that permits fewer stages.

Turbine efficiency η_t is usually defined as the ratio of actual turbine power H_T related to a theoretically possible maximum power without losses:

$$\text{Turbine efficiency } \eta_t = \frac{\text{actual specific turbine power } H_T}{\text{ideal specific turbine power } H_{T,is}}$$

Subscripts: T for turbine
              is for isentropic = no loss

Values of turbine efficiency are between 0.78 and 0.92.

Losses are incurred because of a number of factors such as turning of the flow, friction, leakage between rotating and non-rotating components, tip clearance.

To convey some idea of the magnitude of turbine power, let us consider an example. From velocity triangles of a stage, specific turbine power (i.e. power referenced to unit mass flow rate 1 kg/s) can be obtained. This is done by applying Euler's turbine theorem (which may be used also for a compressor):

Specific turbine power:

$$H_T = u_1 c_{1u} - u_2 c_{2u}$$

u   circumferential velocity of rotating blade
c_{1u}, c_{2u} circumferential component of absolute velocity at rotor
            entry (1) and exit (2)

Usable turbine shaft power is obtained by multiplying specific turbine power by mass flow rate:

$$N_{use} = \dot{m} \, H_T$$

Example: calculate the performance of a turbine stage of the following characteristics:

– rotational velocity n = 12,000 rpm

– mean radius r_1 = 0.5 m

– circumferential component of absolute velocity at rotating wheel entry c_{1u} = 430 m/s

- flow discharging from rotor in axial direction, i.e. no circumferential component of absolute velocity

- mass flow rate $\dot{m}$ = 50 kg/s

Assuming the flow discharges axially from the rotor (c_{2u} = 0), usable turbine shaft power is given by the simple relation:

$N_{use} = \dot{m}\, u_1\, c_{1u}$

Circumferential velocity is the product of radius and angular velocity $\omega = \pi\, n/30$

$$u_1 = r_1\, \omega = \frac{0.5 \times \pi \times 12{,}000}{30} = 628.3 \text{ m/s}$$

Usable turbine shaft power N_{use} then becomes

N_{use} = 50 × 628.3 × 430 kW = 13,508 kW

To account for dimension kW:

$$kW = \left[\frac{kg}{s}\, \frac{m}{s}\, \frac{m}{s}\, \frac{1\,kW}{1000\,W}\, \frac{Ws}{1J}\, \frac{J}{1\,Nm}\, \frac{1\,Ns^2}{1\,mkg} \right]$$

Using the relation 1 kW = 1.34 hp yields

$$N_{use} = 13{,}508 \text{ kW} \times \frac{1.34 \text{ hp}}{1 \text{ kW}} = 18{,}100 \text{ hp}$$

6.1.4 Turbine blade design

Of paramount importance to turbine blade design is the load distribution along the blade length. Blade design generally aims at producing a velocity vector at turbine wheel exit of the same magnitude and direction everywhere along the blade. A non-uniform velocity profile will cause a non-uniform radial pressure distribution with attendant losses due to flow disturbance.

Circumferential velocity is obviously less at the foot of the blade than at the tip. If expansion of the gas were to be restricted to the nozzle guide vane section of the turbine alone, causing the turbine wheel to act as a constant-pressure turbine or impulse turbine as described previously, the relative velocity of the gas would be less at the blade tip than at the foot (this may be easily verified by drawing schematic velocity triangles). Due to a reduced impinging action in the tip area, blade performance would be much reduced there.

For this reason, and to avoid such characteristics, turbine blades are usually designed to be of the constant-pressure type in the foot area, changing gradually to the reaction-type towards the tip (**Fig 6-3**). The added benefit of such design is a higher pressure in the blade tip region

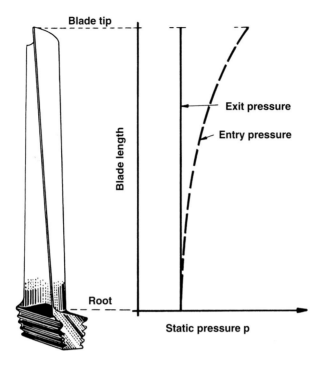

Fig 6-3   Pressure distribution along blade

which will counteract centrifugal forces from rotation, by forcing the flow towards the blade foot.

Optimum turbine performance can be maintained only at or near design rotational speed, as turbine characteristics change markedly with rotation.

The turbine is designed to provide axially-directed flow at turbine discharge. However, a small amount of swirl which is unusable for the generation of thrust will always be present and will constitute a loss. Combatting swirl is usually done by streamlined guide vanes behind the turbine which also act as supporting struts for the rear turbine bearing.

6.2   Turbine assembly – case studies

The turbine rotor is one of the engine components subjected to the highest duty within a turbojet engine. Extreme loads result not only from rotation, but also from operating at high temperatures. Of the utmost importance to turbine improvement is development both of

Fig 6-4   10 stream-
lined supporting
struts shaped to
remove swirling of
flow (Rolls-Royce
Tyne)

turbine materials capable of withstanding higher mechanical and
thermal loads, and, in complement, the improvement of cooling
methods. As materials are exploited up to the maximum tolerable
degree, critical engine parameters such as turbine inlet temperature
(TIT) and rotational speed have to be closely monitored.

We will now look at turbine hardware by analyzing the construction
of the General Electric J79 engine that was once used to power the F-4
and F-104 combat aircraft of the sixties. Many design features of the
J79 are still found in the most modern engines of today.

The rotor of the J79 comprises the rotor disks, blades, and front and
rear stub shafts which transmit turbine loads (**Fig 6-5**).

The conical shaft is designed to transmit mechanical shaft power to
the compressor by a splined end that mates with the rear compressor
shaft. A special connecting bolt locks the components together. At its
rear end the conical shaft is a flange mounted to the first turbine disk
by a number of bolts. All three turbine disks are bolted together
through spacers which also serve to transmit shaft power.

Turbine disks usually feature a tapering wall thickness (with thickness gradually decreasing as the radius increases) to minimize the

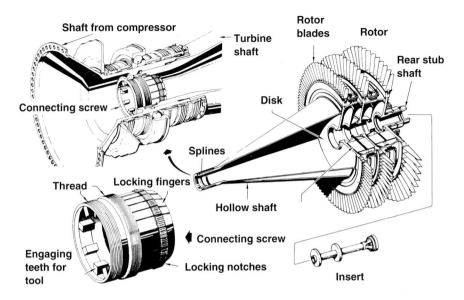

Fig 6-5   Assembly of turbine rotor (General Electric J79)

Fig 6-6   Bolting together conical turbine shaft with front disc. Every two blades form a unit. As a measure against heat, blades have long stem (General Electric CF6)

accumulating centrifugal forces generated when rotating at high speed.

Disks typically have a centre hole, and an outer rim that carries the blades; these are inserted in slots machined into the rim. The blades are held in place by clamps designed to combat vibration and to prevent air leakage. The long shaft of the blades serves to separate the blade root from the hot gas. A sophisticated cooling mechanism provides temperature control between disks.

The increase in operating temperatures to values beyond the melting point of the blade material (1300°C) which has become normal with modern engines, was possible only after progress had been made in sophisticated cooling methods. External cooling alone, by a film of cooling air, proved inadequate; additional cooling had to be provided from the interior of the component. For non-rotating components such as nozzle guide vanes, temperature control methods were relatively straightforward, as was demonstrated by the General Electric CF6 high bypass-ratio engine (**Fig 6-7**).

In order to protect first stage nozzle guide vanes from damage caused by extreme temperatures, the vanes are coated to increase their resistance to material corrosion. Vanes are individually cast and then welded together in pairs. This method ensures that flow leakage is mini-

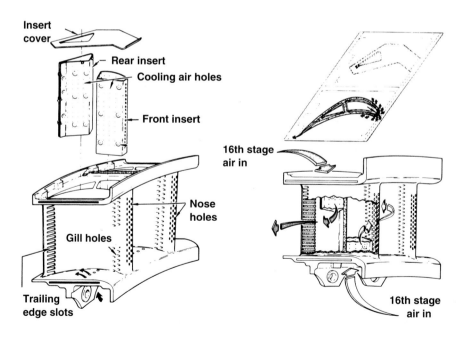

Fig 6-7   Cooling of turbine nozzles (first stage high-pressure turbine nozzle, General Electric CF6)

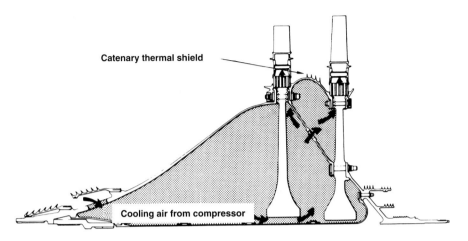

Fig 6-8   Cooling air supply of rotor blades (high-pressure turbine rotor, General Electric CF6)

mized. Also, replacing vanes during maintenance is made easier and is more economical through reduction of time required.

The first stage high pressure nozzle is air cooled by convection, impingement and film cooling.

Vanes are cooled by compressor discharge air which flows through a series of leading edge holes and gill holes located close to the leading-edge on each side. Air flowing from these holes forms a thin film of cooling air over the length of the vane. Internally, the vane is divided into two cavities. Cooling air flowing into the aft cavity is discharged through trailing-edge slots.

Supplying rotor blades with cooling air is much more difficult (**Fig 6-8**). In the case of General Electric's CF6 engine, cooling air initially flows through the conical forward turbine shaft to cool the inside of the rotor and both disks before passing between the paired dovetails and out to the blades (**Fig 6-9**).

A problem associated with the cooling of high-temperature engine parts may arise from small dirt particles contained in the gas. If such particles block a cooling air passage or an exit slot, local over-temperature may lead to catastrophic turbine failure within seconds. In the case of the CF6, rotor blade cooling air, before entering the rotating high-pressure turbine shaft, takes two 180-degree turns, then enters a swirl separator which whirls cooling air in the direction of rotation, thereby causing contaminant particles to be centrifuged outside. The cooling air then passes through a number of dirt traps which utilize centrifugal force to collect and disperse any particles before they can reach the blades.

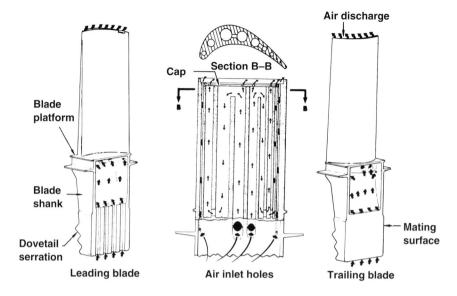

Fig 6-9   Turbine blade cooling detailed (stage 2 high-pressure turbine, General Electric CF6)

The handling of a high-pressure gas stream and preventing losses in the gas path required the development of special seals to minimize flow leakage between the rotating and fixed parts of the turbine. A further aggravation in the sealing task was the thermal expansion of components.

Fig 6-10   Rotating grooves make up moving part of labyrinth seal (high-pressure turbine rotor, General Electric CF6)

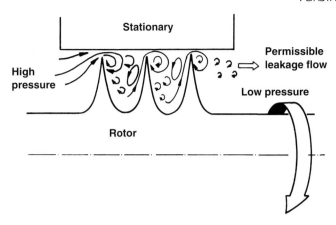

Fig 6-11   Labyrinth seal functioning

The solution to these problems were *labyrinth seals* which are composed of stationary and rotating members. The rotating member is characterized by a number of grooves (the labyrinth) divided by ridges with sharp knife-edged crests. The stationary member incorporates a rub material that allows the rotating knife-edges to cut into the stator, thus providing the required seal. The principle of operation is that a controlled stream of leakage air is allowed to pass through the seal driven by a differential pressure between seal ends. At each knife-edge peak the flow is forced to separate, thereby losing part of its kinetic energy and pressure. The separated flow is temporarily trapped in a groove before entering the next cell of the labyrinth where the process of separation and disturbance is repeated (**Fig 6-11**). By this method of deliberately disturbing the leakage flow, effective sealing is provided at the cost of a small amount of gas flow. Labyrinth sealing is widely used to protect engine bearings from losing lubricating oil.

Labyrinth seal technology is also used at the blade tips of low pressure turbines. The tips of such turbine blades carry a shroud that effectively prevents flow leakage as it rotates with the blade. The added mass at the blade tip necessarily calls for lower rotational speed. Because cooling would be difficult, application of this method is restricted to slower running low-pressure turbines where temperatures are more modest (**Fig 6-12**). Sharp edges at the top of the shrouds form a circular knife which rubs into the soft honeycomb layer mated to the turbine casing (**Fig 6-13**). The operational principle of this form is identical to that of a labyrinth seal designed to minimize leakage.

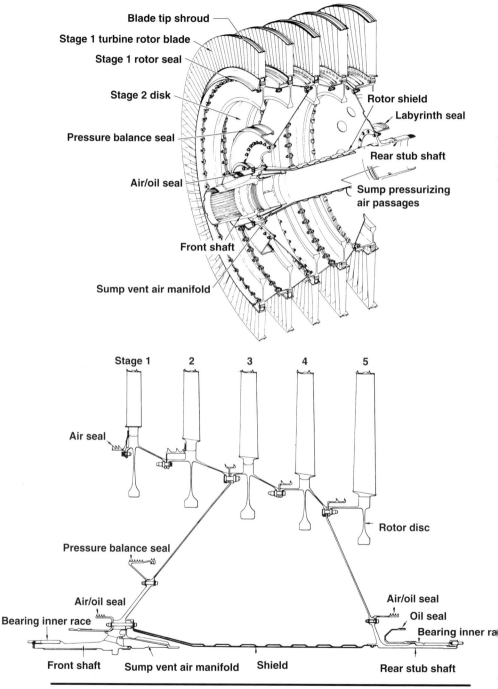

Fig 6-12   Low-pressure turbine to drive fan and low-pressure compressor (General Electric CF6).

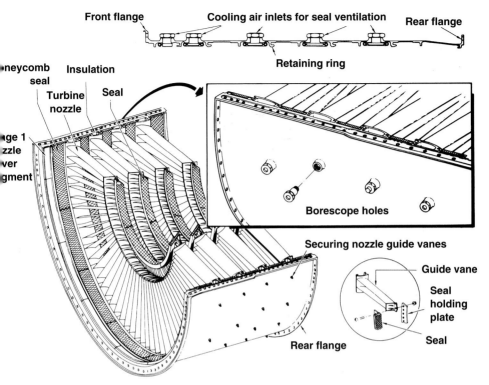

Front flange   Cooling air inlets for seal ventilation   Rear flange

Honeycomb   Insulation   Retaining ring
seal
    Turbine   Seal
    nozzle

Stage 1
nozzle
over
segment

Borescope holes

Securing nozzle guide vanes

Guide vane

Seal
holding
plate

Rear flange   Seal

Fig 6-13   Stator and casing of low-pressure turbine (General Electric CF6)

6.3   High-temperature operation

The principal requirements of a jet engine are high thrust at light weight (i.e. high thrust-to-weight ratio) and low fuel consumption. This is achievable only by increasing turbine inlet temperatures, which over the years were raised at a rate of 10 to 15 degrees per year, from 800°C in 1947 to over 1300°C today.

This progress resulted from improved turbine materials, but above all from advanced cooling methods. To illustrate the effect of turbine inlet temperature on engine performance, specific fuel consumption is usually given as a function of specific thrust (**Fig 6-14**). The graphs shown derive from theoretical cycle analysis, their general message being that by raising turbine inlet temperature, more thrust per unit mass flow rate will be generated. When designing a jet engine, therefore, a high turbine inlet temperature is mandatory for a light-weight engine with a small cross section that makes possible low nacelle aerodynamic drag. The curves also demonstrate that fuel consumption increases with increasing turbine inlet temperature. This effect is

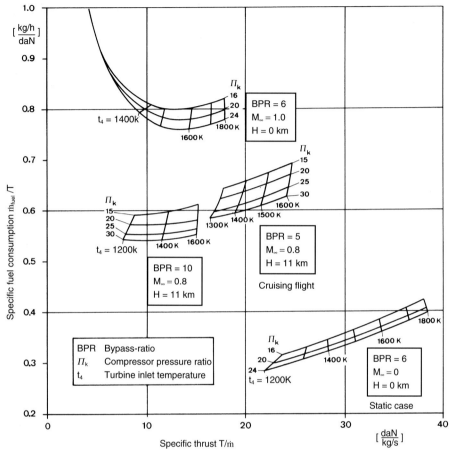

Fig 6-14   Fan performance – influence of turbine inlet temperature t_4, compressor pressure ratio Π_c, bypass-ratio BPR

particularly noticeable for engines of lower bypass-ratio, but not so much for the high bypass-ratio engines found in modern transport aircraft. Because of this characteristic, aircraft equipped with low bypass-ratio engines (i.e. fighters) were once recommended to restrict high temperature operation to only short durations of their flight, such as take-off.

Temperature has different effects on turbine components. The greatest thermal loads have to be sustained by high pressure turbine blades which may eventually fail because of thermal fatigue, oxidation and corrosion.

Thermal fatigue is the term given to the process, caused by cyclic changes of operating temperature, whereby blade material may be caused to fail. At each engine start temperature suddenly rises, causing a temperature gradient to build up rapidly between external and internal portions of a blade. As a result over some length of time, tiny cracks may originate from leading and trailing-edges of the blade which expose damaged areas to metal oxidation. In cases of extreme thermal stress, a blade may even suffer permanent deformation.

One solution to this situation could be the development of new materials better able to sustain high temperatures. Much more promising, however, are advanced cooling methods, even when retaining the material of the blades. It should be remembered that the object of cooling is to keep material temperature within the operating envelope even when the gas temperature is raised.

Is is worthwhile having a brief look at jet engine materials and their properties. Turbine rotor blades, because of their high thermal and mechanical loads, must exhibit high creep strength. Creep is that tendency of a material to undergo permanent deformation when subjected to extreme thermal and mechanical stress, finally ending in catastrophic failure. Metal properties are determined by testing, with standardized specimen subjected to well-defined loadings of temperature and physical stress. The goal of such testing is to determine the (maximum) load combination which can be applied to the material without causing measurable creep.

Choice of the 'right' material is not easy. Metal properties must meet technical requirements, but cost of manufacture is also important. Ideally, a rotor blade should be capable of withstanding maximum permissible physical loads without premature failure from thermal fatigue or oxidation. Alloys must therefore be designed primarily with regard to mechanical stress. A typical rotor blade alloy is NIMONIC 115 by the British manufacturer Henry Wiggin, with the following composition: nickel (Ni, 57.3%), cobalt (Co, 15.0%), chromium (Cr, 15.0%), aluminium (Al, 5.0%), titanium (Ti, 4.0%), molybdenum (Mo, 3.5%), carbon (C, 0.16%), zirconium (Zr, 0.04%), boron (B, 0.014%). In the US, alloys used in turbines bear trademarks such as Udimet700, B1900, Inconel713, Waspalloy, Rene'80.

Basically, metals used for turbine rotor blades are nickel-based alloys which make possible operating times of 50,000 hours.

Blades are usually manufactured by casting or forging. Metal alloys capable of withstanding very high temperatures usually exhibit high resistance to forging. Turbines are therefore, mainly cast. A widely-used method is vacuum casting whereby even the smallest gaseous inclusions in the blade are avoided. Such defects would otherwise cause the material to become brittle and prone to cracks. Because casting affords great precision, blades need not be finished.

The simple blade as cast does not possess the material properties finally required. The necessary strength is provided only after heat treatment where blades are held at a temperature of 1000°C for a couple of hours. During this time, the molecular matrix of the metal is re-arranged into a form which yields the desired properties. In order to prevent the material from oxidation during heat treatment, the process is carried out in an inert-gas atmosphere.

One of the limitations of nickel-based alloys is that they are generally susceptible to oxidation. In this respect, alloys with a high cobalt content are more favourable, but their tensile strength is lower.

A powerful method of combatting material oxidation is by a protective coating made by spraying the blade with a mixture containing pulverized aluminium or chromium, and then heating it to a temperature of 900°C. On the blade surface a layer of nickel/aluminium alloy forms with a thickness of only a few thousandths of a millimetre, sufficient to protect the blade from oxidation and corrosion. Such coatings, on the other hand, are very brittle and may succumb to cracking when hit by solid particles contained in the gas stream. Another problem is that the protective coating may diffuse deeper into the blade at service temperatures above 1050°C, causing the protective effect to diminish. During engine overhaul, the coating of the blades will usually be renewed.

Modern trends aim at replacing metallic materials by silicon-carbides which may permit turbine inlet temperatures as high as 1650°C, their added advantage being lower weight and less cost.

7 Exhaust nozzle

During expansion of the gas in a turbine, energy contained in the gas is extracted and converted into mechanical energy, in the form of shaft power. The amount of energy absorbed by the turbine is only as much as required for driving the compressor and accessories such as the fuel pump, oil pump, electric generator. In engines used for jet propulsion a large proportion of gas energy is still available to be converted into engine thrust. In a *turboshaft* engine the maximum amount of gas energy is extracted by the turbine, whereas in a *turboprop* engine about 90 per cent is extracted for driving the propeller and accessories, leaving the remaining 10 per cent for conversion into thrust.

The task of the exhaust nozzle is to convert gas potential energy into kinetic energy (i.e. gas velocity) necessary for the generation of thrust. This is accomplished solely by the geometrical shape of the nozzle, which is basically a tube of varying cross-section.

Not every nozzle type performs in the same manner. Depending on the type of aircraft, and design flight speed, different types of nozzles are employed. In particular, a distinction is made between convergent and convergent-divergent nozzles.

7.1 Convergent nozzle

It can be shown by simple calculus, that the cross-section of a duct must decrease in the streamwise direction if a subsonic fluid flow is to be accelerated (relevant textbooks of physics). If the duct ends at the smallest cross-section, a convergent nozzle results.

To explain the characteristics of a convergent nozzle, let us assume that a stream of hot gas discharging from the turbine enters the nozzle at a constant total pressure p_{t7}. (Note that total pressure is comprised of static pressure p plus dynamic pressure $q = \frac{1}{2}\rho V^2$.) Because ambient pressure p_0 is lower than static pressure p_7 at the nozzle entry, the flow will accelerate to exit velocity V_7 (**Fig 7-1a**). Let us further assume static pressure p_7 at nozzle discharge to be exactly equivalent to ambient ($p_7 = p_0$), so that the gas completely expands.

Ambient pressure is not a constant but decreases with altitude. If the aircraft flies at high altitude, lower ambient pressure will cause exhaust velocity V_7 to increase accordingly. This process cannot go on indefinitely, however. There is a limit when the jet discharges at sonic

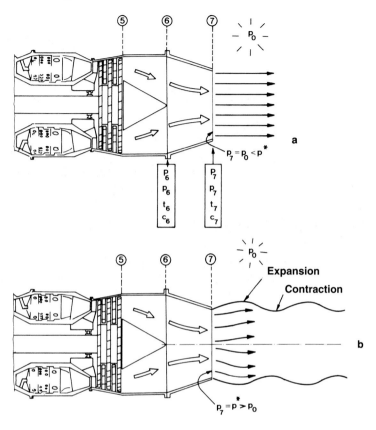

Fig 7-1   Flow in a convergent nozzle
a) subcritical operation
b) supercritical operation

velocity. Static pressure at nozzle discharge is then said to be *critical*. If ambient pressure continues to decrease (because the aircraft flies at higher altitude) then conditions at nozzle discharge will remain unaltered. When nozzle mass flow rate is at its maximum, the nozzle is said to be 'choked', i.e. mass flow cannot be increased any more.

When a jet is discharging from the nozzle at a higher static pressure than ambient pressure, its expansion is incomplete or *under-expanded*. As a result pressure will rapidly equalize causing the jet to expand in (an undesirable) radial direction, with particle inertia now causing pressure in the middle of the jet to fall below ambient. Underpressure will then trigger contraction of the jet such that a zone of over-expansion is succeeded by a zone of under-expansion (**Fig 7-1b**). In this case, jet efficiency with regard to thrust is low.

A convergent nozzle of fixed geometry is used for aircraft flying at

Fig 7-2   Common nozzle of fan flow and core engine (Pratt & Whitney JT8D
powering Boeing 727)

subsonic (or low supersonic) velocities. The most frequent application
is with high-subsonic commercial and military transports.

Because these aircraft exclusively employ turbofan engines, the
choice of mixing the hot and cold gas stream may determine the design
of the convergent nozzle. At times when bypass-ratios of engines were
low (up to about 1.5 was typical for engine technology of the sixties)
the gas was expanded in a common nozzle. This was the case, for
example, with Pratt & Whitney's JT8D engine that was built in large
quantities to power the Boeing 727 and early 737 jets.

Rather than ducting both gas streams coaxially, Rolls-Royce
designed a nozzle with an internal mixer that forces the cold bypass
flow through a number of oval slots and so causes both streams to mix.

Engines of higher bypass-ratio frequently feature separate exhaust
nozzles for the cool fan flow and the hot core flow.

These nozzle designs were developed primarily in the sixties, but
their principles are alive in the most modern engines of today. The
choice of design is driven by nozzle weight, nacelle aerodynamic drag,
nozzle efficiency, and noise. A rear cone protruding from some nozzle
designs is aimed at allowing external expansion of the (otherwise
under-expanded) jet to generate additional thrust forces on the cone.

Fig 7-3   Mixing of fan flow with core engine flow (Rolls-Royce Spey)

Fig 7-4   Separate nozzles for fan flow and core engine flow (Rolls-Royce/Snecma M45H, aircraft VFW614)

7.2   Convergent/divergent nozzle

Convergent nozzles are used primarily for subsonic flight speeds, but may be employed also at low supersonic Mach numbers, up to Mach 1.5. For higher exhaust velocities a different nozzle shape is required. The geometric characteristic of this nozzle is a decreasing cross-sectional area in its forward part (much like a convergent nozzle), followed by a cross-sectional increase in its rearward portion (the divergent section). Such nozzles were employed in steam engines in the last century and bear the name of their Swedish inventor, Laval (**Fig 7-5**).

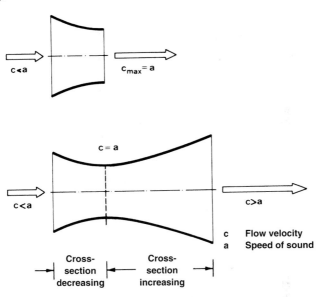

Fig 7-5 Comparison of convergent nozzle for subsonic jet with convergent/divergent (Laval) nozzle for supersonic jet

In its convergent (forward) section, flow in a Laval-type nozzle behaves as previously described, i.e. continuous acceleration in the duct up to sonic velocity which is reached in the nozzle throat (where the cross-section is smallest). In the divergent section, pressure is allowed to decrease below its critical value, with fluid velocity continuing to accelerate to supersonic values.

The decisive parameter is the area ratio of nozzle exit area A to nozzle throat area A*. Specific selection of the area ratio allows any pressure ratio to be achieved (**Fig 7-6**).

In practice, a fixed-geometry supersonic nozzle is badly suited for aircraft applications because the exhaust area cannot be matched to

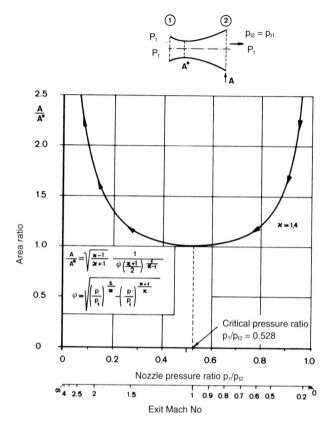

Fig 7-6   Ideal gas flow nozzle

the varying conditions of ambient pressure and engine power settings. Furthermore, such nozzles would be long and heavy. For this reason, engines using thrust augmentation feature variable-geometry nozzles of sometimes complicated construction, but of short length.

Of the many types possible, there are mainly two types of variable-geometry nozzle that have found widespread application, the *ejector* nozzle and the *iris* nozzle.

Ejector nozzle

In design the ejector nozzle features a convergent *primary nozzle* which is enclosed concentrically within a tube (**Fig 7-7**). The hot exhaust flow from the engine attains sonic velocity at the nozzle exit ($M_1 = 1$), the highest Mach number possible with a convergent nozzle. Because of its high pressure, the jet will expand radially after exiting from the primary nozzle to supersonic Mach numbers ($M_1 > 1$). Driven by suction from

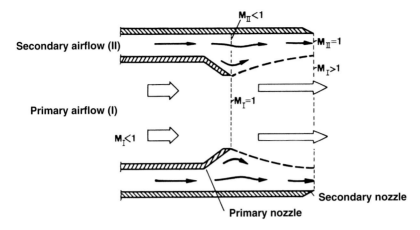

Fig 7-7   Variable-geometry nozzle and fixed ejector

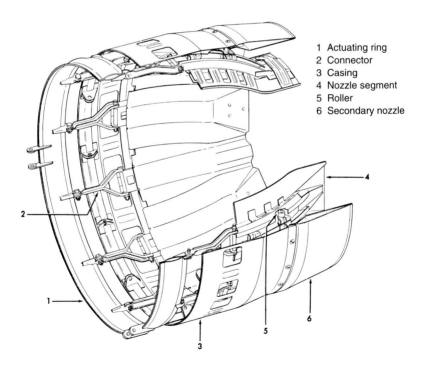

1 Actuating ring
2 Connector
3 Casing
4 Nozzle segment
5 Roller
6 Secondary nozzle

Fig 7-8   Ejector nozzle (General Electric J85 turbojet)

the primary gas-stream, a secondary flow is induced, the main task of which is to smooth the primary jet and thereby allow it to continuously accelerate to supersonic velocity. Without a secondary flow, the primary jet would rapidly expand to ambient pressure by bursting. In this case losses would be high and thrust low. Secondary flow, while damping the primary jet, is itself accelerated to sonic velocity at the nozzle exit ($M_{11} = 1$).

The divergent section of the ejector nozzle is practically formed by a gaseous stream which at the same time provides a shielding to the nozzle outer casing, thus effectively preventing the hot gas from contacting the nozzle body.

The ejector nozzle exists in a number of variants. In its simplest version it constitutes a fixed ejector of slightly divergent cross-section which encloses a variable-geometry primary nozzle. Such a nozzle was mounted to the augmentor tube of the General Electric J85 engine (**Fig 7-8**).

Variation of exit cross-section is accomplished by translating the nozzle axially with hydraulic actuators. Rollers of the ejector nozzle run in tracks of the primary nozzle segments. When the fixed-geometry nozzle is fully retracted, primary nozzle exit cross-section is a minimum. Conversely, when the fixed-geometry nozzle is fully extended, primary nozzle exit area is a maximum.

The benefits of this design are lightweight construction and trouble-free operation. The operational characteristics of this nozzle are essentially those of a convergent nozzle with limited supersonic performance and acceptable aerodynamic drag at subsonic speeds. Because it is not a high-performance nozzle, its application is restricted to relatively simple combat aircraft.

A much more efficient nozzle, albeit of more complicated construction, is the *variable flap ejector* nozzle (**Fig 7-8**). The convergent section of the nozzle comprises a number of overlapping segments, while the divergent section is formed by a secondary flow which is ducted around the core engine and exits through a variable-geometry nozzle. As both parts of the nozzle are of variable-geometry design, area ratio may be ideally adjusted to varying flight conditions, although at the expense of a more complicated and heavier construction. Of disadvantage is the large amount of secondary air required which results in high aerodynamic drag.

Even more sophisticated is the *blow-in door ejector* nozzle which utilizes 'tertiary' air sucked in from outside, near the fuselage aft end (**Fig 7-12**). At high supersonic flight speed, the blow-in doors are closed because of the higher interior pressure; the secondary nozzle exit is in the fully open position. If flight speed is decreased to low supersonic velocities (around Mach 1.2), pressure in the nozzle is decreased automatically causing a gradual reduction of exit cross-section. This process

Fig 7-9   Nozzle closed (top) and open (bottom), achieved by translating ejector ring (Northrop F-5 combat aircraft)

continues until the nozzle segments reach a stop at the minimum design exit cross-section. The aircraft is still in the transonic speed regime (between Mach 0.8 and 1.2). If flight speed is further reduced, pressure inside the nozzle will drop accordingly until the spring-loaded tertiary doors open, allowing air from outside to be sucked in. This nozzle

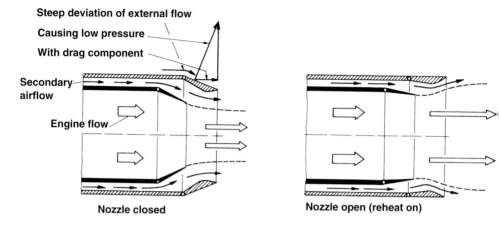

Steep deviation of external flow
Causing low pressure
With drag component
Secondary airflow
Engine flow

Nozzle closed   **Nozzle open (reheat on)**

Fig 7-10   Fully adjustable ejector nozzle

Fig 7-11   Adjustable secondary nozzle (General Electric J79)

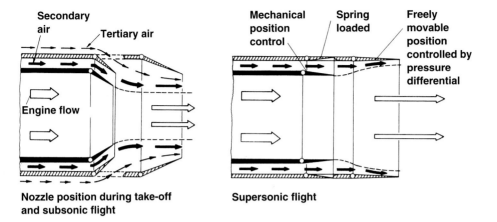

Fig 7-12   Ejector nozzle with tertiary inlet doors

Fig 7-13   Ejector nozzle with tertiary inlet doors

configuration is maintained throughout the subsonic flight regime and for landing.

Sucking-in considerable amounts of tertiary air requires flow ducts to be aerodynamically of high quality to keep losses low. Because of its favourable characteristics both at subsonic and supersonic flight Mach numbers, the ejector nozzle has found widespread application with supersonic aircraft, for example F-111, Viggen, Concorde, Tu-144, and SR-71.

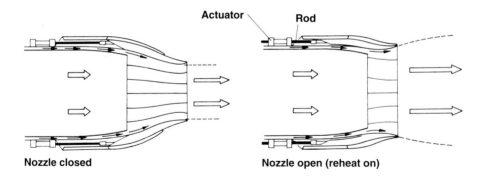

Fig 7-14   Iris nozzle

Iris nozzle

Although of greater mechanical complexity, the iris nozzle excels by superb aerodynamic cleanliness. Axial translation of the nozzle segments is accomplished through rods actuated by hydraulic jacks. The construction permits any required nozzle exit cross-section to be attained (**Fig 7-14**).

Fig 7-15   Iris nozzle contributes to superb performance of combat aircraft (test flight of Grumman F-14, iris nozzle at smallest exhaust area)

Variable-geometry nozzles designed for supersonic flight speed generally incur high aerodynamic drag at subsonic velocities which must be overcome by additional thrust. High drag levels result from turning the external flow abruptly when the nozzle is at its minimum cross-section. Zones of low pressure resulting from bending of the flow act against the direction of aircraft motion (**Fig 7-17**). The favourable shape of the iris nozzle allows the flow to pass smoothly along the nozzle contour with only little risk of flow separation.

The iris nozzle resulted from large-scale research by NASA and US aircraft manufacturers. It is considered to be one of the most efficient nozzle shapes, and enjoys widespread application to supersonic military aircraft such as F-15, F-16, B-1B, and F-14.

7.3   Reverse thrust

As most aircraft land at speeds in the order of 130 kt (250 km/h), long runway distances are required for the ground roll down to taxying speeds. Apart from high landing speed, aircraft weight, and the limited capacity of mechanical wheel brakes compound the slowing-down problem.

Increasing brake capacity could be possible by enlarging the brakes, but this would cause added aircraft weight and space. Also, on a wet runway braking action will be impaired anyway, regardless of brake capacity.

It appeared logical, therefore, to use the energy in the propulsion system to slow the aircraft down. The result is the thrust reverser which frequently is an integral part of the exhaust system.

The thrust reverser functions by obstructing the exhaust by blocker doors which can be turned into the flow. These divert the jet radially outwards and with a markedly forward velocity component. Turning the exhaust flow to a forward direction results in a forward thrust component which acts as a brake (**Fig 7-16**).

In practice, the design of a particular thrust reverser depends on the engine with which it is used. In all cases the engine will be of turbofan type.

If a common nozzle is used both for fan and core streams, the thrust reverser will capture all of the flow (**Fig 7-17**). When not in use, the reverser's internal surfaces must align with the duct in order not to disturb the flow. The harmonious integration of the reverser into the overall nozzle design is therefore of great importance.

In the case of high bypass-ratio engines with separate exhausts for core and fan jets, two separate reversers may be employed as was demonstrated by the General Electric CF6 engine in the DC-10

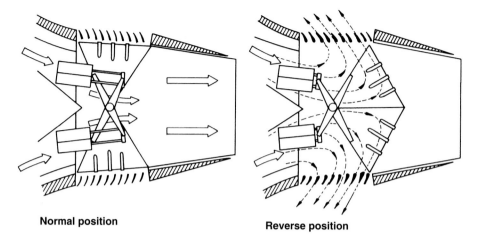

Normal position   **Reverse position**

Fig 7-16   Thrust reverser operation

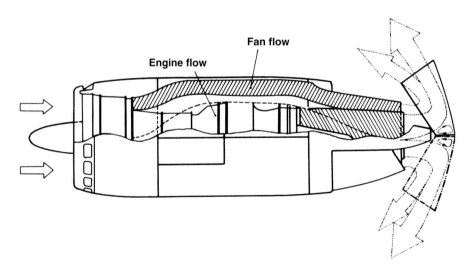

Fan flow

Engine flow

Fig 7-17   Thrust reverser operation of turbofan with common exhaust nozzle
(Pratt & Whitney TF33, aircraft Lockheed C-141 Starlifter)

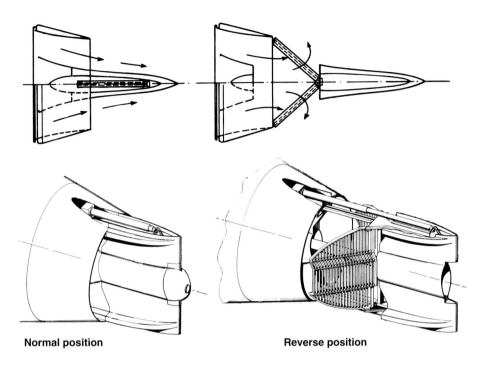

Normal position   **Reverse position**

Fig 7-18   Thrust reverser for core engine flow of a high bypass-ratio engine
(General Electric CF6)

transport aircraft (**Fig 7-18**). In their retracted position, core reverser
cascades are covered by a shroud that aligns with the duct. Reverser
action is achieved by sliding the shroud backward, and then swinging
cascades into the jet flow by means of a spindle drive. The cascade
material is heat resistant Inconel 718, that of the shroud lightweight
titanium.

Reversing a fan jet is accomplished by cascades arranged as single
elements around the engine circumference. In their retracted position
they are shrouded on both sides in order not to disturb the interior and
exterior flows (**Fig 7-19**). All components must fit tightly to prevent
flow leakage in their stowed position which would otherwise cause
aerodynamic drag. The shroud, together with the rear nacelle, forms
the (convergent) nozzle for the fan jet. When extended into the reverse
position, the cascade shroud will first slide backwards before the 16
individual blocker doors swing into the fan nozzle duct and direct the
fan flow through the fixed cascades. The shape of the grid turns the
flow to exit in a forward direction so providing reverse thrust. The
process of activating reverse thrust takes 2 seconds, which is a good

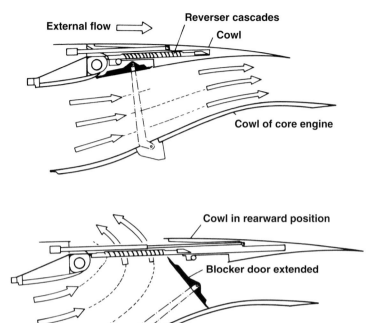

Fig 7-19   Thrust reverser for fan flow of a high bypass-ratio engine. After translating cowl backwards, flow guiding cascades for reverse operation are
exposed (General Electric CF6, aircraft McDonnell Douglas DC-10)

value given the machinery involved. On the other hand, a longer time
would be unacceptable for the task required.

Generally, thrust reversers are employed only with subsonic transport aircraft for reducing their landing run. Supersonic combat aircraft
employ braking chutes for the same purpose, or simply rely on wheel
braking. The major reason that precludes thrust reversers being used
on combat aircraft are weight and the space needed for the construction. One exception to this rule is the Swedish Viggen, a veteran combat
aircraft of the early seventies, but a good example of integrating a
thrust reverser with an ejector nozzle.

In the retracted position, three thrust reverser plates are integrated
into, and form part of, the ejector nozzle wall. The thrust reverser is
activated by undercarriage compression. Activation is by hydraulic
jacks which have to be cooled because they operate close to the hot
exhaust gas stream.

Fig 7-20   In their
retracted position,
impinging plates are
flush with nozzle (SAAB
Viggen)

Fig 7-21   On icy
runways, Viggen's
thrust reverser proves
useful. Three impinging
plates are hydraulically
operated. Actuators
must be cooled, with air
exit holes visible

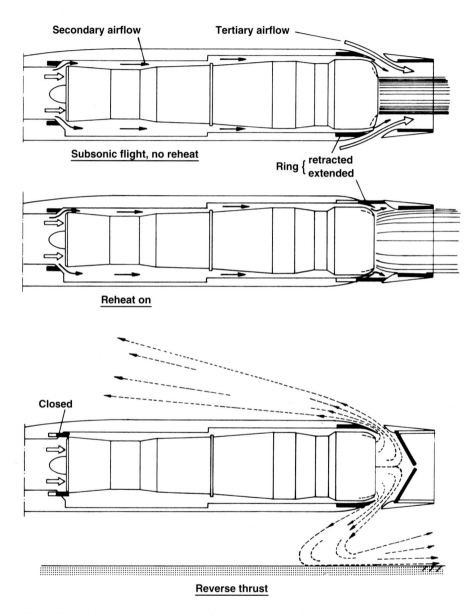

Fig 7-22 Using the ejector nozzle for reverse thrust (Viggen)

The function of the ejector nozzle slot is twofold:

- at take-off and during subsonic flight, tertiary air is ingested through the slot to provide thrust augmentation (**Fig 7-22** top)

- after touch-down, all of the jet flow exhausts through the slot (**Fig 7-22**, bottom); the rounding of the fuselage contour also assists the reversed jet remaining attached to the fuselage (Coanda effect)

- in supersonic flight with reheat on, the ejector nozzle slot is closed by a ring-shaped cover sheet that extends from the fuselage to slide over the slot (**Fig 7-22**, centre)

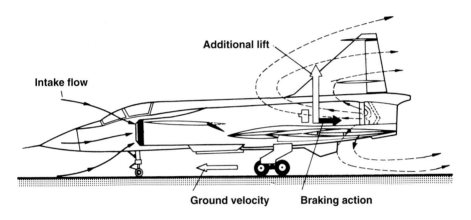

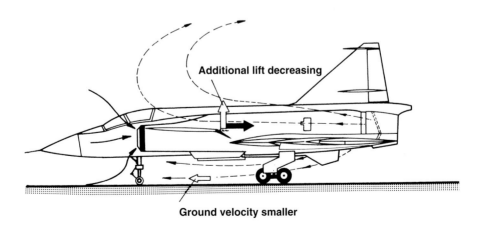

Fig 7-23   Effect of reversed jet on Viggen aircraft at high and low aircraft ground velocity

An aircraft is inherently not well suited to reverse thrust operation. If a decision is made for a reverser, possible unfavourable effects have to be considered. In the case of the Viggen aircraft, for example, the reversed jet, apart from its braking action, causes a zone of low pressure on the wing upper side immediately after touch-down, plus a marked ground vortex. Both phenomena cause a nose-down pitching moment which tends to lift the aircraft's tail (**Fig** 7-23, top). As a result, action of the wheel brakes is impaired through an effectively reduced aircraft weight and, additionally, the aircraft shows a tendency to leave track. Although the effect lasts only for a couple of seconds until speed has dropped to an uncritical value, the pilot has to be prepared for the occurrence. Thereafter, the resulting aerodynamic force of the reversed jet on the airframe is moving forward, with the tail-down pitching moment low enough to be easily dealt with by the pilot (**Fig 7-23**, bottom). The hazard of ingesting the reversed hot jet through the main intake may be relieved by opening the primary nozzle so that the reversed jet ejects at a steeper angle.

Smart use of reverse thrust will allow the aircraft even to roll backward to facilitate parking on limited ground space (as in parking a car).

The different types of thrust reverser shown raises the question as to the essential requirements for thrust reverser design. A well-designed reverser should be capable of reducing the aircraft's landing run by at least 30 per cent. This requires 50 to 70 per cent of max take-off thrust to be available for reverse. Forces resulting from reverse thrust must be sustained by the reverser construction, irrespective of whether the reversed jet is hot or cold. Reverser structural weight must be low. When not in use, the nozzle must not disturb the main flow; when in use, the reversed jet must not be allowed to enter the air intake.

8 Thrust augmentation

In some cases it is necessary to increase thrust above the engine's normal thrust level. The reasons are as follows:

When taking-off from reduced-length runways, or on a hot day, a safe lift-off speed must be achievable. For combat aircraft, additional thrust must be provided for manoeuvring flight.

Higher thrust can readily be provided by more powerful engines. However, for combat aircraft in particular, heavier weight and short-period operation preclude installation of such engines. In practice, thrust augmentation is accomplished by applying *reheat* which has become a characteristic feature of all supersonic aircraft. In civil aviation *water injection* was used up to the seventies to increase take-off thrust, until the advent of high bypass-ratio turbofan engines, with their ample thrust reserves, rendered the method obsolete.

8.1   Reheat

A very effective and widely-used method of increasing thrust is by reheat or afterburning which enables thrust to be raised by 50 per cent. When the afterburner is lit, its flame in the jet exhaust becomes visible

Fig 8-1   Reheat can increase thrust by 50 percent and more (McDonnell Douglas F-4 combat aircraft powered by two General Electric J79 turbojets

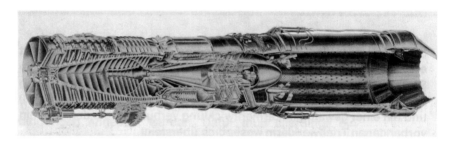

Fig 8-2   Basically, thrust augmentation is accomplished by a tube-like combustion chamber mounted aft of the original engine (General Electric J79)

and the noise grows to values far beyond the already high noise level of the 'dry' engine.

With the exception of the Concorde supersonic airliner, reheat is employed only by military supersonic aircraft. For combat aircraft reheat is of great importance not only, for example, to accelerate the aircraft quickly in the interdiction/strike role, but to escape safely from the combat arena if this is the better choice. Another reason to equip (supersonic) aircraft with reheat is to reduce the take-off run.

Higher supersonic flight speeds became possible only with reheat. While at first applied only to military aircraft, early attempts proved successful also in the civil market, as shown by the Concorde and the then Soviet Tu-144 (which is no longer flying). Noise regulations will probably bar reheat from any future civil applications.

The technology of reheat makes use of the fact that the hot gas, after passing the turbine, still contains sufficient quantities of oxygen to allow a second combustion given an appropriate injection of fuel again. (It will be recalled that only part of the air discharged by the compressor is used for combustion, the greater proportion being used for cooling purposes.)

By reheating the jet exhaust the flow attains a higher level of energy available for expansion in the exhaust nozzle. The result is a higher exit velocity, a prerequisite for achieving more thrust (as indicated by the momentum theorem, *cf* Chapter 2).

In principle, the afterburner is a tube-like structure attached to the gas generator immediately behind the turbine. The forward part is designed as a diffuser (i.e. cross-section increasing) which lowers flow Mach number from 0.5 to 0.2, to prevent the flame from being carried away by a flow that is too fast.

Particularly noteworthy is the simple construction of the afterburner assembly, which is comprised of only four major components (**Fig 8-3**):

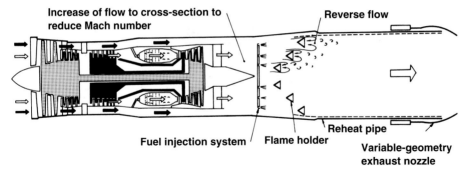

Increase of flow to cross-section to reduce Mach number

Reverse flow

Fuel injection system **Flame holder**

Reheat pipe

Variable-geometry exhaust nozzle

Fig 8-3   Typical of afterburners is a relatively straightforward assembly (schematic of Volvo RM8 turbojet for the Viggen combat aircraft)

flame tube

fuel injection system

flame holder assembly

variable-geometry exhaust nozzle

One component, the exhaust nozzle in its various types, has already been dealt with in the previous section. When afterburning is not in operation, the nozzle is configured to its smallest exit cross-section. Should the exhaust nozzle accidentally open to full cross-section, pressure would immediately drop causing thrust to collapse.

The central part of the afterburner assembly is the afterburner duct where combustion takes place. The duct contains a number of heat-resistant liners which are linked to the outer casing through tracks and a self-locking mechanism (**Fig 8-4**). Because of the heat, multiple slots are provided through which cooling air from the flow path between the casing and the flame tube is arranged to flow into the flame tube. As a precaution against oxidation, the flame tube is ceramically coated. At the downstream end of the flame tube is the variable-geometry nozzle. For the purpose of adjusting nozzle position, hydraulic actuators are mounted on the outer casing.

A fuel injection system, separate from that of the engine, is employed to supply and distribute the reheat fuel. Fuel is distributed through manifolds to spray bars which extend radially inward, the fuel being sprayed into the gas stream through a number of holes arranged to provide intense mixing.

One item not expressly mentioned in the list of major components, but always visible on cutaways or photos, needs some explanation, namely the *rear cone*. Shaped as an elliptic axisymmetric body, the rear

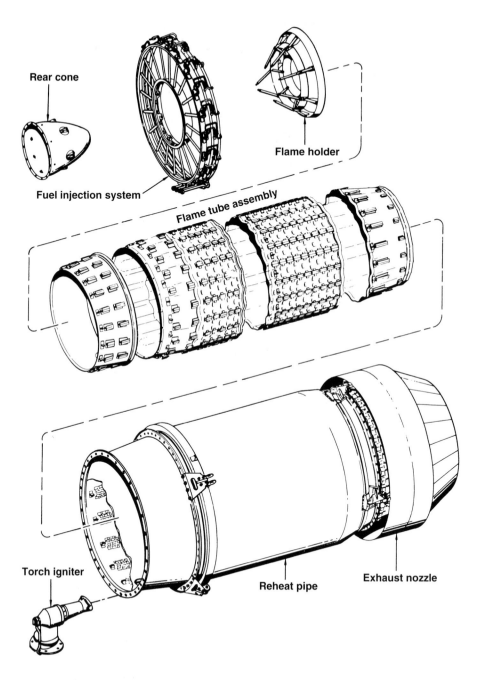

Fig 8-4   Afterburner assembly (General Electric J79)

Fig 8-5   Upstream view of afterburner of J79 turbojet, with secondary nozzle in foreground and primary nozzle inside, both fully open

Fig 8-6   Fuel injection system of General Electric J79 turbojet

Fig 8-7   Flameholder mounted to rear cone; V-shaped cross-section of flameholder rings to assure reverse flow for flame stabilizing

cone serves many purposes. First, the gas flow from the turbine is a
cylindrical shape which must be gradually fitted to occupy the full cross
section of the afterburner flame tube. Hence, the task of the rear cone
is essentially of a fluid dynamic nature.

Secondly, the rear cone acts as a supporting structure to the spray
bars (which are not of a mechanically rugged construction).

Finally, the rear cone carries the flame holder, an essential part in
the afterburner architecture. Because of the high temperature in which
it operates, the rear cone is ceramically coated.

The flameholder is located downstream of the fuel injection nozzles.
Usually it is made up of three concentric rings of V-shaped cross-
section. Even though the velocity of the gas stream has been reduced
by the diffuser-like entry section of the afterburner tube, flame propagation speed is still less than flow velocity, so the flame would be
carried away. It is the task of the V-section flameholder rings to
generate eddies and local reverse flows where the flame can stably rest.
(**Fig 8-5**) The effectiveness of afterburning is increased by using a
concentric group of flameholder rings. In order to prevent the burner
tube from choking, the rings are staggered.

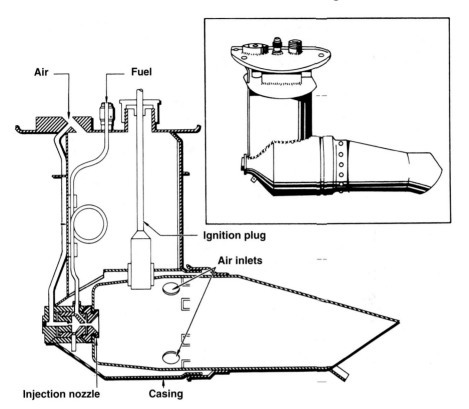

Air — Fuel

Ignition plug

Air inlets

Injection nozzle   Casing

Fig 8-8   Torch igniter (General Electric J79)

The afterburner control mechanism is complex, comprising a separate fuel system with fuel pump, fuel filter, and fuel control, plus an ignition system. Igniting the afterburner is automatic once the pilot selects afterburner position at the throttle.

Despite the high temperature of the gas, ignition of the fuel/air mixture is usually not automatic of itself. Willingness of the gas to ignite depends to some extent on flight altitude and Mach number. To ensure ignition under all conditions, an independent ignition source is provided.

Ignition methods may differ. Early engines utilized 'hot shot ignition', by injecting additional fuel into the combustion chamber and behind the turbine, allowing the flame of the combustion chamber to penetrate through the turbine into the afterburner tube. As turbine blades operate at their upper temperature limit, this method could be used only for short periods.

A frequently used method to light the afterburner is by a *torch igniter* which is permanently burning whenever the afterburner is in use

(**Fig 8-8**). By this method the afterburner is kept in permanent readiness to ignite, independent of altitude and of Mach number.

The use of an afterburner cannot be viewed as economically advantageous. The increase in specific fuel consumption far outweighs the gain in thrust. Fluid dynamic losses are imposed by the flameholder and the fuel injection tubes, and also by skin friction. Even if the flow were frictionless, a loss in total pressure would be incurred due to heating.

Nevertheless, afterburning is considered to be the only practicable method of achieving high and very high flight Mach numbers. Newer developments aim at keeping the flame tube extremely short.

8.2   Water injection

This is a method which was widely used in civil aviation up to the seventies, but is now history. We will briefly look at the underlying principle.

According to the theorem of momentum, thrust depends not only on the increase of airstream velocity, but also on mass flow rate (Chapter 2). As mass flow rate is linked to air density (mass = density × volume), a variation of properties of the air will cause thrust to be increased.

According to the equation of state for an ideal gas:

$$\rho = \frac{p}{Rt}$$

with ρ density, t static temperature, p static pressure, R gas constant, density will increase with pressure, but decrease with temperature. This explains why thrust is less at airports located high (low pressure), for example in South America, or on hot days even at airports at sea level. Engine manufacturers take these effects into account in their manuals by giving thrust characteristics as a function of ambient temperature (**Fig 8-9**). Graphs in general show loss of thrust with increase of temperature. For example, the Pratt & Whitney JT3D-5 engine that powered Boeing 707 and McDonnell Douglas DC-8 transports, generates 9070 kgf (20,000 lb) of thrust at sea level and 15°C temperature (point A), but only 8550 kgf (18,850 lb) at 30°C temperature on the same airport, a deficit of 6 per cent in otherwise identical conditions. As a result, either the take-off run will have to be increased, or the payload of the aircraft lowered, to accommodate the unfavourable temperature or altitude effects.

Now for the water injection method to increase thrust:

The temperature of the engine airflow can be lowered by injecting water upstream of the compressor. As the water vaporizes, tempera-

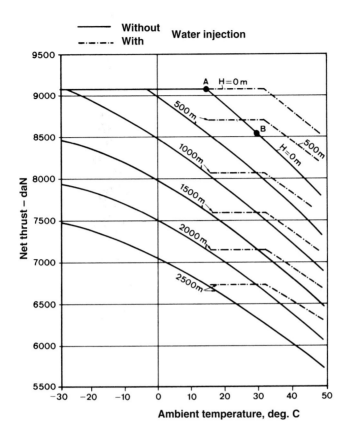

Fig 8-9 Static thrust characteristics – effect of water injection (Pratt & Whitney JT3D-5, typical low bypass-ratio turbofan used for transport aircraft of the sixties)

ture will drop causing density, hence mass, to increase, which directly provides additional thrust due to increased mass flow rate.

With the advent of high bypass-ratio engines, and their large amounts of take-off thrust, water injection was superseded by technological progress. But it constituted an interesting episode in the quest for higher thrust.

9 Engine systems

Accessories and engine systems are indispensable devices to make the engine function properly. They are usually mounted at the perimeter of the engine and occupy the space between engine casing and nacelle (**Fig 9-1**).

We know from a car engine that it can only perform properly if the fuel pump delivers sufficient fuel, the carburettor is properly adjusted, and the ignition provides sparks at correct times. A turbine engine functions in much the same manner, with the added requirement for high component reliability in order to ensure flight safety.

A system is defined as an integrated entity made up of diverse parts that function together to perform a required task. For a turbine engine the following major systems are essential:

- A fuel system

- A lubrication system

- A starter system

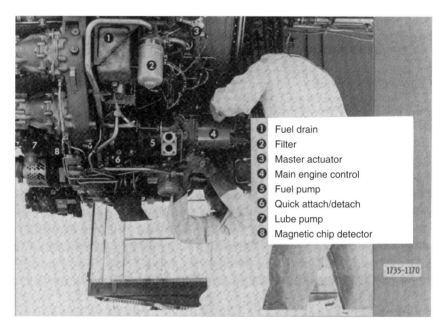

❶	Fuel drain
❷	Filter
❸	Master actuator
❹	Main engine control
❺	Fuel pump
❻	Quick attach/detach
❼	Lube pump
❽	Magnetic chip detector

1735-1170

Fig 9-1 Accessories (General Electric CF6)

- An electric system
- A cooling and sealing air system
- A display system.

In addition, other systems may also be installed depending on the type of engine and aircraft, such as:

- A thrust reverser system
- A fire protection system
- A de-icing system

Systems pertaining particularly to supersonic aircraft are:

- An afterburner fuel system
- A nozzle area control system
- An air-intake control system.

9.1   Fuel system

It is the task of the fuel system to supply the engine with the required amount of fuel, suitably processed for orderly combustion, for any operating condition such as starting-up, acceleration, cruising flight at altitude, rapid climb to altitude etc.

In general, the fuel system comprises a fuel supply system, a fuel control system and relevant valves and piping. A distinction is made between the *airframe-supplied* and the *engine-supplied* components of the fuel system. The airframe-supplied parts consists of fuel tanks, fuel pumps, and devices to indicate and command engine operation such as instrumentation and control levers (**Fig 9-2**). The engine-supplied part of the fuel control system consists of fuel pumps, the fuel control system, burners and piping.

Fuel is conveyed from tanks to the engine by suitable pumps (fuel boost pumps) which are electrically-driven to provide a low-pressure fuel flow for the engine-supplied fuel system. Fuel pressure is in the range of 1 to 2.5 bar (14 to 35 psi). On its way to the engine, the fuel is filtered. Fuel flow is measured by a fuel flowmeter, its reading being indicated on the cockpit instrument panel.

After fuel is pumped into the engine-supplied fuel system, pressure will be markedly increased. High pressure of the fuel is necessary to achieve adequate fuel spray quality from the spray nozzles in the combustion chamber. Pressure is increased in two steps:

A low-pressure fuel pump raises fuel pressure up to 7 bar (100 psi),

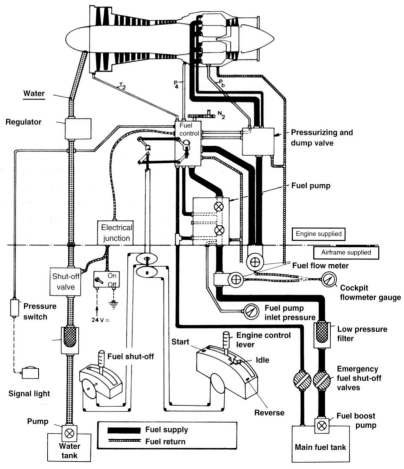

Fig 9-2   Fuel system of turbofan engine of the sixties (Pratt & Whitney JT3D)

then the fuel is pre-heated by passing through an air/fuel heat exchanger, and filtered again in a high-pressure filter. In a second step, pressure is boosted to 80 bar (1,140 psi). Fuel is then pumped to the fuel control unit from where distribution to the burners is made.

9.1.1   Fuel pumps

The supply of fuel from the wing fuel tanks is accomplished by low-pressure pumps which are electrically-operated and run at high rotational speed. Such pumps function like a radial compressor and work as an immersion pump.

In the engine-supplied fuel system, two types of pumps are used to provide high-pressure fuel flow: axial piston fuel pumps for very high pressure, and gear-type fuel pumps for low pressure.

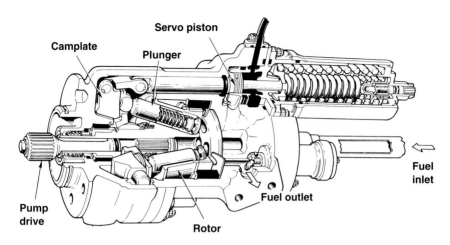

Fig 9-3   Plunger-type fuel pump for very high pressure

Axial piston fuel pumps
In the high pressure section of the fuel system, plunger-type fuel pumps
are used. Such pumps convert the rotary motion of an input shaft into
axial reciprocating motion of pistons (**Fig 9-3**).

Power to operate the pump is provided directly from the engine,
through the accessory gearbox. The quantity of fuel pumped depends
on engine rpm and piston stroke. Typical quantities are in the range of
400 to 8,000 litres per hour (105 to 2,130 gallons/h) at a maximum
pressure of 140 bar (1,960 psi). The power requirement for driving the
pump is up to 80 hp.

Reciprocating motion is usually accomplished by rotation of an
angled cam plate. As the plate rotates, the pistons reciprocate, taking
in fuel when moving away from the inlet ports, and expelling it when
pushed forward by the angled cam plate. The length of stroke varies
with cam plate inclination which is controlled by a servo piston, biased
by springs to give the full stroke position of the plungers. As this piston
is subjected to servo pressure on the spring side, and pump delivery
pressure on the other, variations in the pressure equilibrium cause the
servo piston to move, thus altering cam plate inclination and, therefore, pump stroke.

Gear pumps
Gear-on-gear pumps consist of two gears, usually of equal size, that
mesh with each other inside a housing (**Fig 9-4**). Rotation of the driving
gear rotates the second gear. Fuel is conveyed in the space between
teeth. A safety valve allows excess fuel to return if delivery pressure
exceeds a limiting spring load.

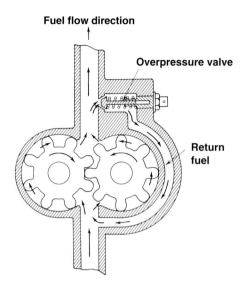

Fig 9-4   Gear-type fuel pump

The advantage of gear pumps is their low weight and high delivery rate. Gear pumps are used in the engine-supplied fuel system.

9.1.2   Fuel control unit

Engine control is accomplished by varying the fuel flow to the injection nozzles. To obtain increased thrust, fuel pressure is first increased so that more fuel can be injected. The resulting increase in gas temperature will also increase the gas velocity through the turbine section. The ensuing increase in turbine speed will increase the engine mass flow rate and hence the thrust.

The interrelation of fuel injected and thrust generated is complicated by atmospheric conditions, in particular variations in temperature and pressure. Both result in variations of density which directly affects thrust.

It is the task of the fuel control unit to provide the engine with fuel in a form suitable for combustion, in all atmospheric conditions, so that a preselected thrust level can be maintained.

This is different from a car engine where the driver directly controls engine power with the throttle pedal. In a turbine engine, the pilot indirectly commands engine thrust by a throttle lever position which acts as a signal to the fuel control unit. Fuel control then calculates the required fuel flow, taking into account various critical parameters, and adjusting fuel flow to the engine in a way such that neither overheating nor engine stall will occur. In order to be able to accomplish this calculation, more information to the fuel control unit is needed, which may comprise the following list of input parameters:

1 Control lever position as input from pilot
2 State variables of intake discharge airflow, i.e. compressor inlet temperature t_t, compressor inlet pressure p_t
3 Rotational speed of all rotors
4 Rate of change of rotational speed.
   (Note: to prevent the compressor from surging, acceleration of the engine must comply with the operating instructions given by the manufacturer, which must be independent of power lever movements by the pilot.)
5 Compressor discharge pressure of the high-pressure compressor
6 Engine pressure ratio (EPR), i.e. p_{t7}/p_{t2}
7 Burner pressure
8 Turbine inlet temperature (TIT) of the high-pressure turbine, or alternatively:
   Exhaust gas temperature (EGT)
   (Note: although blade wear is largely affected by turbine inlet temperature, it is easier to measure exhaust gas temperature, which is related to TIT.)

The classical fuel control units are hydromechanical devices. Modern units are 'full authority digital electronic control' units (FADEC) which incorporate multiple control tasks.

Engine control requires a primary control parameter to be selected. In modern high bypass-ratio engines such as the CF6, rotational speed of the high-pressure compressor (N_2) is the preferred choice.

Engine control is accomplished by keeping N_2 speed constant for a selected throttle lever position (i.e. high-pressure rotor), regardless of varying ambient conditions. Control of the low-pressure rotor (comprising fan, low-pressure compressor and low-pressure turbine) is through aerodynamic coupling to the high-pressure rotor.

The advantages of using the N_2 parameter for control are that:

– rotational speed can easily be measured

– measurement is independent of aircraft altitude or engine operating condition

– accuracy of measurement is good

– rotational speed is a good indicator of thrust (which cannot itself be measured in flight)

Low bypass-ratio engines (and early pure jet engines) use engine (total) pressure ratio p_{t9}/p_{t2} (usually abbreviated EPR) as the primary control parameter. This parameter is also a reliable indicator of thrust, which may be thought of as the product of pressure and cross-sectional area. The major disadvantage of using the EPR parameter is that pressures cannot be measured as exactly as rotational speed.

Although basically applicable to high bypass-ratio engines, the EPR method would in fact be more complex there, because the thrust both of the fan and the core engine streams would have to be calculated separately.

The operational experience of the airlines led to the formulation of requirements for a modern control system. Additionally to providing engine control, such an advanced control unit should incorporate a central computer capable of the following tasks:

1 to perform power control modes, at least for critical cases such as take-off, maximum climb, maximum cruise;
2 to harmonize engine thrust on multi-engine aircraft so that individual engine thrust should not deviate more than ±0.2% from a preselected average, independent of flight speed, altitude and aircraft attitude;
3 to allow either constant engine rotational speed or constant flight speed to be selected as the prime control parameter at the discretion of the pilot;
4 to be of modular construction to facilitate easy replacement of faulty components, or of the complete unit, in less than one hour;
5 ease of accessibility after opening the engine cowling.

For the control task itself, the following requirements were established:

a) engine spooling-up from flight-idle to max take-off thrust in less than 5 seconds, at flight speeds below 270 km/h (145 knots). This case is important for go-around or missed approach situations.
b) time between max take-off thrust to max reverse in less than 6 seconds, which is important for aborted take-off.
c) time between flight-idle thrust to max reverse thrust in less than 5 seconds, which pertains to daily operating practice.

These requirements were established in the seventies for a future control unit. Today, with *full authority digital engine control* (FADEC) the common practice on modern engines, these requirements are met.

9.1.3   Spray nozzles

Last in the functional chain of the fuel system, spray nozzles (burners) have the task of processing fuel in a way such that efficient burning is accomplished. A prerequisite for achieving a homogeneous fuel/air mixture for burning is vaporization of the fuel, followed by intense mixing of the fuel vapor with the airstream from the compressor. The

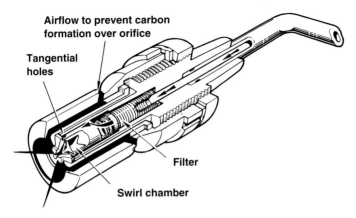

Airflow to prevent carbon formation over orifice

Tangential holes

Filter

Swirl chamber

Fig 9-5   Simplex burner

length of the combustion chamber is determined by this process.

Basically, vaporization is achieved by passing the fuel into a swirl chamber where tangentially arranged holes impart swirl to the fuel particles. These then emerge from the spray nozzle not only in an axial, but also in a lateral direction by virtue of centrifugal forces from the swirl, forming a typical spray cone.

This method was first used in *Simplex* burners of early jet engines (**Fig 9-5**). Operation was satisfactory at high fuel flow rates and high pressure. At low fuel pressure, and at high altitudes, with the engine running at low power, the shape of the spray cone was inadequate for burning fuel efficiently. The reason was that fuel flow rate increases with the square of fuel pressure. Therefore, optimizing spray nozzles for low pressure fuel flow would have required an enormous fuel pressure for high fuel flow rates, which could not be provided by pump technology in those early years.

A more satisfactory operation is achieved with a *Duplex* burner featuring two separate fuel feeds and separate coaxial nozzle exits (**Fig 9-6**). At low fuel pressure, fuel is ejected only from the smaller primary nozzle, which provides good vaporization through a better match of low fuel pressure and size of orifice. As fuel pressure is increased, a pressure operated valve progressively admits fuel to the main fuel supply line, resulting in a second spray cone which then issues from the main nozzle.

9.1.4 Jet engine fuels
Unlike a high-performance piston engine that will not operate properly if serviced with low-octane fuel, a gas turbine engine is much more tolerant of fuel quality. Fuels must however, conform to strict requirements to give optimum engine operating performance.

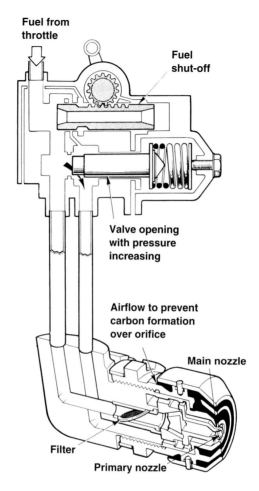

Fig 9-6   Duplex burner

In view of the broad range of the aircraft operating envelope, extending from normal ambient conditions at take-off and landing to low atmospheric pressure and temperature at cruising altitude, fuel requirements are, for example:

- calorific value must be high

- combustion must be efficient at all conditions

- engine start and in-flight relight must be easily possible

- fuel and combustion products must not cause above-average engine deterioration

- fuel must possess sufficient lubrication properties for movable parts within the fuel system, such as fuel pumps
- fuel must be easy to handle, store, and pump, in particular at low airport temperatures.

The easy handling of fuel depends on viscosity, which is a function of temperature. Fuel is required to be thin enough for being easily pumped into aircraft fuel tanks. As there is always some water content in the fuel, ice crystals will form at low temperatures and may clog filters and fuel lines. As a precaution, fuel may be heated or charged with additives.

For ease of starting, positive ignition of the fuel/air mixture must be possible after the engine has been spun-up to ignition speed by the engine starter. Fuel readiness to ignite depends doubly on fuel quality: first from its property to be volatile, i.e. to evaporate, in particular at low temperatures; second, from the degree of vaporization (size of fluid particles) which depends on fuel viscosity, fuel pressure and the design of the spray nozzle.

The *calorific value* determines the heat content of the fuel which would be released by complete combustion. In the International System of units, this value is given by the term 'Kilojoule per kilogram mass of fuel', i.e. kJ/kg.

A distinction is made between gross and net calorific value. The *gross calorific value* of the fuel additionally contains the (latent) heat of evaporation of the water that is formed when burning hydrocarbons. The heat of vaporizing 1 kg of water at 20°C temperature is 2,450 kJ, i.e. this amount of heat will be lost due to the inevitable evaporation of the water.

Subtraction of the loss due to water evaporization, gives the *net calorific value*. This value is usually taken for calculations. The net calorific value of average turbine fuels is

$$H_n = 42,000 \text{ kJ/kg}$$

In the British system of units, the calorific value is given in British Thermal Units (BTU) referenced to one pound of fuel weight, i.e. BTU/lb. Alternatively, calorific value sometimes is referenced to one Imperial Gallon, i.e. BTU/Imp Gal.

Using the relationship

1 British Thermal Unit = 1,055 Joule

the net calorific value in the British System of Units may easily be found:

$$H_n = 42,000 \frac{kJ}{kg} \times 1 \frac{BTU}{1.055 \text{ kJ}} \times 0.4536 \frac{kg}{1 \text{ lb}} = 18,057 \frac{BTU}{lb}$$

The amount of fuel required for a given amount of heat released is less with a high calorific value. Therefore, fuel calorific value directly affects aircraft range.

The corrosive action of fuel and its combustion products depends on the sulphuric content. By burning sulphur, its dioxide SO_2 forms and this, together with water, combines to form the aggressive sulphuric acid. As sulphur is an inherent part of any hydrocarbon fuel and cannot be completely removed, its maximum allowable content must not exceed 0.4%.

If water is found in fuel tanks it can be removed. However, as fuel absorbs moisture from the air, such water cannot be removed.

Different requirements for jet engine fuels have led to typical fuel standards for military and civil aviation, i.e. kerosine-type fuels (JET A-1, JP-5, JP-6, JP-7) and wide-cut fuels (JP-4).

Turbine engine fuels are refinery products from crude oil, which differ mainly in freeze point, volatility and flash point. Low volatility, for example, is required for high-performance military aircraft which climb rapidly to altitude, but must not suffer fuel loss from low ambient pressure evaporation. For these aircraft the JP-4 fuel standard was specified. Aircraft operating on aircraft carriers use fuel of the JP-5 standard which calls for a higher flash point of 60°C.

As aircraft speeds increased to high supersonic Mach numbers, fuels were needed which were thermally stable. By this is meant fuels having the capability of absorbing heat without producing carbon deposits in the heat exchanger or at fuel nozzles. Such a property is particularly important where fuel is used to cool parts of the airframe that are heated by skin friction, as in the case with the SR-71 high-speed reconnaissance aircraft. For such aircraft JP-6 and JP-7 fuel standards were developed.

In civil aviation, Jet A-1 fuel is used with a freezing point of minus 50°C. This specification was developed particularly for long-haul high-subsonic transport aircraft on transatlantic flights.

9.2   Lubrication system

The rotating components of a turbine engine require a number of bearings which must be reliably supplied with lubricating oil (**Fig 9-7**). Bearings are both of roller and of ball type. Roller bearings are able to carry radial forces only, whilst ball bearings carry both longitudinal and radial forces. When under load, bearing temperature will rise, and microscopic particles of metal may break from the bearing surfaces.

Oil serves multiple purposes in a turbine engine: to lubricate and cool bearings, and to wash away metal particles. A lubrication system,

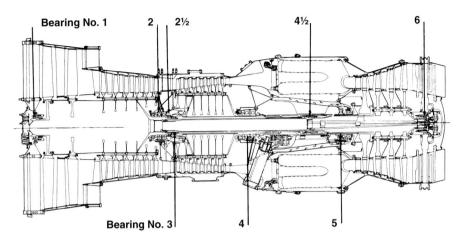

Bearing No. 1   2   2½   4½   6

Bearing No. 3   4   5

Fig 9-7   Ball and roller bearings that must be lubricated (Bearing locations of Pratt & Whitney JT3D)

designed in most cases as a *dry sump* system, usually comprises four sub-systems:

lube oil supply

lube oil scavenge

oil seal pressurization

sump ventilation.

Lube oil supply
The lube supply sub-system consists of the oil tank, the lube and scavenge pump, lube discharge nozzles, and related lube supply plumbing. In modern engines, such as the General Electric CF6, lube and scavenge pumps form compact units mounted on the accessory drive gearbox (**Fig 9-1**). These pumps are exclusively of the gear type (**Fig 9-4**).

High-pressure oil from the pump is forced through a filter before being discharged from the pump unit. During cold starting, oil is directed through a filter bypass valve to allow for the greater viscosity at low temperatures. Oil leaving the pump is then routed through the lube supply lines to the discharge nozzles located in the main shaft bearing areas, accessory gearbox and other parts of the engine where lubrication is vital.

The oil tank is flexibly mounted to alleviate the effects of vibration. The unit can be easily removed and disassembled for cleaning. As a fire-preventative measure, oil tank material is silicon-coated.

The integral tube and scavenge pump is located in a cool, accessible environment for greater reliability and ease of maintenance. Check valves in the pump permit removal of the filter element without loss of oil.

Lube scavenge system
The lube scavenge system comprises the scavenge section of the integral lube and scavenge pump, a scavenge oil filter, a fuel/oil heat exchanger, and related plumbing. Oil from the different bearing sumps, and from the gearbox, is suction drawn to the pump, and directed through a master chip detector for early detection of any metal particles in the oil. The oil is then pumped to the oil filter, fuel/oil heat exchanger and finally back into the oil tank.

Oil seal pressurization
Pressurized air from the fan compressor is used to prevent oil from leaking through seals, and to cool bearing sumps. Internal air passages are designed in a way such that the air flow through the seals counteracts the tendency of the oil to leak through them (**Fig 9-8**). Oil sumps may be encased in protective air jackets to prevent excessive heat from

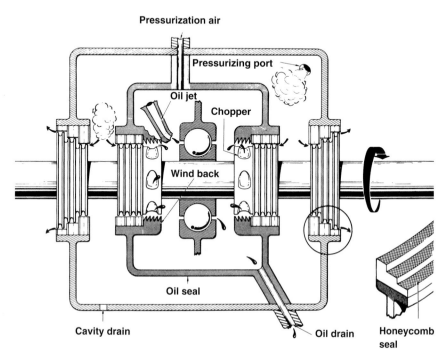

Fig 9-8   Functioning of sump sealing (General Electric)

reaching the oil-wetted sump walls and prevent the oil from coking or from deteriorating. Thread-like patterns of seal cavities counteract oil leakage through seals during engine start before pressurized air becomes available.

Sump ventilation
This subsystem comprises the plumbing necessary to remove the air from engine sumps and to vent it overboard through tubing in the low-pressure turbine shaft.

Jet engine lubricating oils
The steady increase in the loads and operating temperatures of the bearings necessitated the development of synthetic lubricating oils that did not originate from crude oil. The major benefit of such oils is a near-constant viscosity down to temperatures as low as −40°C where a thin condition can be maintained.

9.3   Electric system

Electricity is required for a variety of tasks on a turbine engine, such as ignition, measurement and monitoring.

Ignition system
The primary task of the ignition system is to ignite the fuel/air mixture in the combustion chambers. A secondary task is the relight capability following engine malfunction. Ignition is also used continuously as a precautionary measure during critical phases of a flight such as take-off, during landing approach, when flying through exceptionally bad weather or in turbulence.

  For safety reasons, engines are equipped with two ignition systems operating independently of each other. As fuel/air mixtures are reluctant to ignite, the generation of powerful sparks is essential. High voltage, however, causes excessive wear on electrodes, which therefore need to be replaced after (typically) 100 hours of service life.

Electric measuring and monitoring devices
Instruments requiring electricity for operation are as follows:

1   Exhaust gas temperature gauge (EGT)
     A number of thermocouples may be arranged evenly around the circumference of the engine casing behind the high-pressure turbine. From the temperatures measured, an average value will be calculated and then indicated in the cockpit.

2   Tachometer of the high-speed rotor, N_2
This device usually functions without external energy. The electric signal generated is proportional to engine rotational speed.

3   Tachometer of the low-speed rotor, N_1
The sensor requires voltage to generate a magnetic field. The passage of a fan blade disturbs the magnetic field so resulting in electric pulses proportional to engine speed **(Fig 9-9)** The accuracy of measurement is very high. In high bypass-ratio engines, N_1 is used as a thrust setting parameter.

4   Fuel pump pressure gauge
5   Entry pressure gauge of low-pressure turbine
6   Engine pressure ratio (EPR) indicator
7   Oil pressure gauge
8   Scavenge oil temperature gauge
9   Oil quantity measuring device
10   Oil filter pressure drop indicator
11   Fuel flow indicator
12   Fuel temperature behind fuel/oil heat exchanger gauge
13   Fuel low pressure gauge
14   Pressure drop across fuel filter gauge
15   Starter valve position indicator.

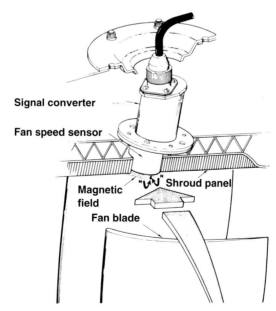

Fig 9-9   Measuring fan speed N_1

9.4   Starting system

The lowest rotational speed at which a turbine engine can continue running, is termed *engine idle*. Usually, for speeds below idle, a separate starter motor is required for engine cranking.

Depending on type of engine and aircraft, a variety of starter types is available. Military engines, in particular, require a minimum time for starting, which must also be performed independently of external

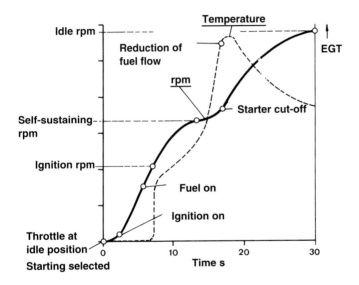

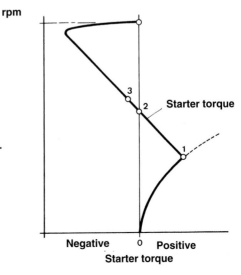

Fig 9-10 Starting procedure indicated by engine rotational speed, temperature and starter torque

3   Starter cut-off.
2   Self-sustaining rpm.
1   Ignition

equipment. Starting requirements for civil engines is less demanding, but should be possible in less than 30 seconds.

9.4.1   Engine starting

Engine start is initiated by setting the throttle to *ground idle* position and switching on the starter. The starting cycle then continues automatically. The task of the pilot is to monitor the relevant cockpit instruments.

When the starter motor has cranked up the engine to about 8 per cent of ground idle speed, ignition is switched on (**Fig 9-10**). Engine speed then increases further, while airflow through the engine grows accordingly. After reaching the lowest possible air mass flow rate for ignition, fuel will be injected. This sequence prevents unburned fuel from accumulating in the engine and being expelled through the exhaust nozzle.

Engine light-up is indicated on cockpit instruments by a rise in exhaust gas temperature (**Fig 9-10**, 1). The engine then begins itself to produce torque, but still requires support from the starter (1–2). When the starter motor curve crosses the zero-torque line (2), the engine has reached its self-sustaining speed, i.e. where engine torque equals

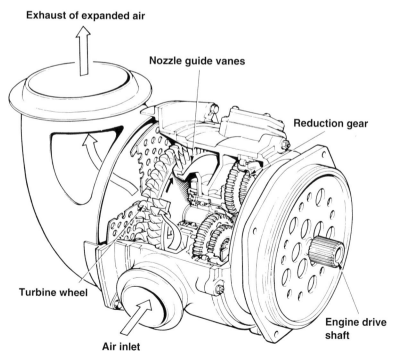

Fig 9-11   Air-turbine starter

starter motor torque. Only then is the engine power sufficient to accelerate the engine to ground idle speed. During this phase, the starter motor will be cut out (3) and fuel flow adjusted (i.e. reduced) to flight idle.

If ignition or starter motor is accidentally switched off before self-sustaining speed is achieved, as can happen with (older) engines having no automatic starting system, engine speed will drop, but temperature will rise enormously (hung start).

In general, it is beneficial if the starter motor continues to contribute to engine rotation long enough to cut down the starting period, as engine and starter combined will reach ground idle speed much faster. The starter motor should not be cut off before the fuel control unit has begun reducing fuel flow to the amount necessary for ground idle.

9.4.2   Types of starters

As a starter motor is activated only for a short period relative to the duration of a flight, the most important design requirement is maximum starting power at minimum weight. Additional requirements are operational reliability, low maintenance costs, simple construction.

Various types of starter have been developed over the years, eg:

- air-turbine starter

- electric starter

- gas-turbine starter

- cartridge starter

Air-turbine starter

Civil jet aircraft engines are almost exclusively started by an air-turbine starter (**Fig 9-11**). The system consists of a high-speed constant pressure turbine, reduction gear, pawl coupling, shut-off valve plus related plumbing and electric cables.

The reduction gear transforms high-speed low torque into low-speed high torque necessary for cranking the heavy rotor assemblies and the accessories. Air exhausts through special exits in the engine cowl.

The advantage in this type of starter is its low weight (10 to 15 daN, i.e. 20 to 30 lb), but the air requirement is high and requires a separate pressure supply source. This is usually an airborne auxiliary power unit (APU), another engine already running, or an external ground supply unit. The APU is the most frequent supply source.

The design requirements call for a minimum of 5,000 starting cycles after which the starter must still function perfectly. To facilitate maintenance, the starter is mounted on the accessory drive, using quick attach/detach technology (QAD).

Electric starter
The electric starter basically corresponds to the type well known from car engines. The system consists of the electric starter motor, reduction gear, driving jaw, and overload protection. Because of its high electric power demand and its weight, the electric starter is used only in smaller turbofan engines, turboprop engines and turboshaft engines (helicopter engines, APU).

A combined usage of starter and power generator for electricity is occasionally envisaged. It is also considered a possible solution with some future military transports.

Gas-turbine starter
This type resembles a small turbine engine complete with fuel system, starting and lubricating system. The compact gas generator consists of a centrifugal-type compressor, reverse flow combustion chamber, and a single-stage axial turbine to drive the compressor. Gas from this gas generator drives a free turbine which, through a reduction gear, drives the engine.

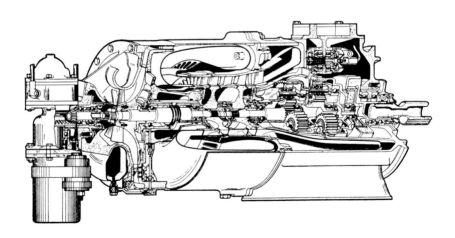

Fig 9-12   Gas turbine starter (Lucas)

The gas-turbine starter constitutes a technical milestone, but due to weight, complexity and costs could not survive in modern aviation.

Cartridge starter
Operating in the same way as the air pressure starter, a cartridge starter generates gas for driving a starter turbine. Triggered by electrical ignition, the cartridge burns for a period of 15 seconds to generate a high-pressure, high-temperature gas for driving an air turbine.

The low weight of the unit and its high torque are attractive features of the cartridge starter. Three cartridges are available before the system must be reloaded. Because of this deficiency, starting from an external source, or from the airborne APU, must also be possible.

9.5   Engine monitoring and operation

The turbine engine, although of straightforward operation, constitutes a complex system which requires adequate monitoring to ensure flight safety. To this end related instruments and controls are available to the pilot. During the years of a three-crew cockpit layout (which ended in the eighties), it was the task of the flight engineer to monitor fuel flow and engine systems. This task is now either automated or integrated in the two-crew cockpit concept.

Instruments may be classified in three categories:

- engine performance

- fuel and oil monitoring

- special tasks

Engine performance
Instruments (or electronic displays) that indicate engine performance are mounted on the main instrument panel to be readily visible by the pilot. These instruments convey vital information on rotational speed of high-pressure and low-pressure spools, engine pressure ratio (EPR) and exhaust gas temperature (EGT).

Thrust is impossible to measure directly in an aircraft, because it would require the engine to be freely mounted. Instead, engine pressure ratio may be used. Alternatively, rotational speed of the fan, N_1 is used on high bypass-ratio engines, and presented as a percentage of nominal speed.

Fuel and oil monitoring
For monitoring fuel and oil status, indicators for quantity, pressure and temperature are used.

Fig 9-13 Cockpit of a modern airliner (Airbus A320)

Fig 9-14 At the times of the three-crew cockpit, it was the task of the flight engineer to monitor fuel and engine systems (early Boeing 747)

Fuel flow indicators display fuel consumption in kg/h or lb/h. Fuel flow indicating the amount of fuel that is fed to the burners is of fundamental interest to the pilot. Complementary indications are fuel quantity available, and fuel used.

A temperature sensor permanently monitors tank fuel temperature.

A warning light alerts the pilot to low fuel temperature, as water content in the fuel could turn into ice that could clog fuel filters. The formation of ice is countered by heating the fuel by passing it through a fuel/air heat exchanger.

Oil supply to critical parts of the engine such as bearings, is vital for safe operation. This requires constant monitoring of oil pressure. Additionally, oil quantity and oil temperature may be indicated in the cockpit. At low oil pressure, an alarming light will alert the pilot, which is also the case if the oil filter is bypassed at low oil temperatures during engine start.

Special tasks
The fast running rotors of the engine must necessarily be well balanced. Unbalance may result from failure of rotating parts, or even loss of a blade, causing the engine to vibrate. If not counteracted immediately, the engine could fail catastrophically. Vibration is, therefore, constantly monitored during engine operation.

Engine handling
Controls for engine operation in a modern commercial transport aircraft are arranged on the central pedestal – in much the same way as twenty years ago. What is new, however, is that the pilot selects one of five throttle lever positions, with each position assigned to a typical phase of the flight such as:

- maximum thrust for take-off (most forward position)
- flexible take-off thrust (if take-off is made at a lower aircraft weight)
- climb thrust (reduced thrust to comply with noise regulations)
- idle
- reverse thrust

After the pilot has selected a throttle lever position, the *full authority digital engine control* (FADEC) calculates the required thrust and initiates the necessary input for smooth engine running. This process is fully automatic.

Additionally, at the discretion of the pilot, the throttle lever may be operated in the traditional way, which may be useful in some special cases.

10 Environmental considerations

Apart from the task for which they were conceived, many industrial products generate side effects which are unwanted, but unavoidable. When such effects give rise to public concern, remedies have to be sought in the form of technical solutions that eliminate or minimize the annoyances.

The gas turbine aero-engine, conceived as a prime mover for propelling aircraft, needs the Earth's atmosphere for functioning – like man who needs the same atmosphere for living. The environmental effects of the jet engine are noise and exhaust emissions, features that are external to the engine and do not bear directly on the purpose of propelling the aircraft.

10.1 Noise

The single most annoying factor causing community concern is engine noise which in severe cases may be perceived as injury.

Noise impression

Energy conversion within the jet engine, necessary for the generation of thrust, requires large masses of air to be processed. Part of the energy is absorbed by oscillations of air molecules that give rise to sound waves. Although the energetic content of sound waves is small, propagation is unconstrained and only lightly damped.

Classical parameters to characterize sound are *frequency* and *intensity*. Frequency denotes the number of oscillations per unit time, usually expressed in Hertz = 1/s (1 Hertz = 1 oscillation per second). Intensity is considered to be an objective physical quantity that defines the noise impression. It is a measure of the acoustic power emitted from a source, and is frequently expressed in the dimension of Watts per square metre (W/m^2).

Because measures of the auditory magnitude include subjective effects, there is no universally accepted method for describing noise. However, it is generally accepted, that acoustic intensity is composed of a number of frequency bands, each of which causes different subjective responses in the auditory system. In order to arrive at meaningful physical data, broadband noise is classified into critical bands which contribute in a specific way to the loudness of a sound.

One of the measures of auditory magnitude of noise to include subjective effects is termed *perceived noise level*, defined as:

$$PNL = 10\,\frac{\log PN}{\log 2} + 40$$

Perceived noise level (PNL) is a nondimensional logarithmic parameter derived from *perceived noisiness* PN. The value of 40 represents the auditory magnitude of a standard noise source (PN = 1) perceived by normal speech. The unit of perceived noisiness PN is the decibel, commonly written PNdB.

To the human ear, a doubling of perceived noisiness PN will not be felt as a doubling of perceived noise level PNL. This is because noise level is expressed on a logarithmic scale. For example, doubling perceived noisiness from a value of 1 to a value of 2, i.e. PN = 2, yields a perceived noise level of PNL = 50, a further doubling to 4 yields PNL = 60. Because of the subjective nature of judging annoyance due to noise, more sophisticated parameters are invoked which weight frequency bands for noise intensity, duration, and number of events over a specified time.

The PNdB unit was created with specific reference to aircraft noise annoyance. The noise spectrum is divided into discrete frequency bands which are weighted with regard to subjective effects to include scales of loudness, speech interference and perceived noise level PN.

The unit recommended by the International Standardization Organization (ISO) to describe the noise on the ground produced by aircraft is the *effective perceived noise level* (EPNL). Numerical values are given in decibels and written as EPNdB. This unit is in widespread use for aircraft certification.

Noise certification
A newly designed airliner must comply with the noise certification rules contained in Annex 16 of ICAO (International Civil Aviation Organization). In the US, the largest producer of civil aircraft, noise regulations are given in FAR part 36 (FAR = Federal Aviation Regulation). Usually, noise certification is made according to FAR, which is now complemented by the European Joint Airworthiness Requirements (JAR).

In the noise standards, maximum permitted noise in terms of effective perceived noise levels are specified for the *flyover, sideline and landing* conditions as a function of aircraft weight (**Fig 10-1**). More specifically, new commercial aircraft must produce not more than 108 EPNdB (value dependent on take-off gross weight) at three measuring points, namely:
On the approach, at a point one nautical mile (1.85 km) before the

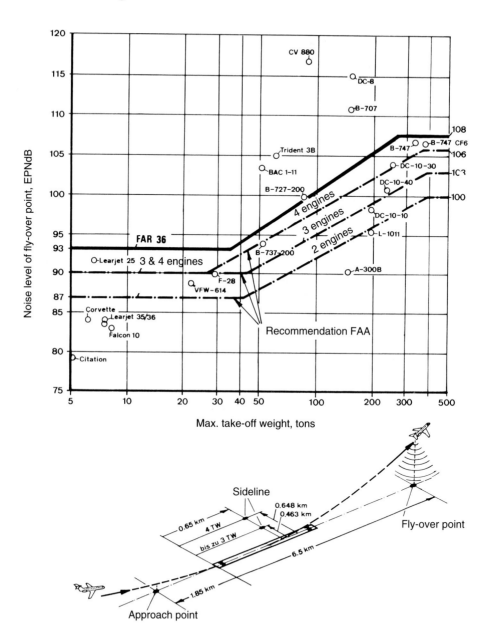

Fig 10-1   FAR 36 noise regulations

runway threshold, on the approach centreline, the aircraft being at a height of 113 m (370 ft);

On take-off, at a point 6.5 km (3.5 nautical miles) from brake-release, regardless of altitude;

On take-off, at a point to the side of the runway centreline, depending on the number of engines:

- 460 m (0.25 nautical miles) for two- and three-engined aircraft (A330, B777, MD-11);

- 650 m (0.35 nm) for four-engined aircraft (B-747, A340).

Since the introduction of FAR 36 in 1970, substantial noise reductions have been accomplished, largely due to high bypass-ratio engines which rendered noisy low bypass-ratio engines obsolete.

Aircraft noise sources

A gas turbine engine is characterized by a unique noise spectrum which unequivocally results from its specific design. Basically, all components of the engine contribute to engine noise, i.e. fan, compressor, combustion chamber, turbine, exhaust section. The relative magnitude of different noise sources can vary not only from engine to engine, but also with operating conditions.

Typically for the plain turbojet engines of the past were a small cross-section, relatively small air mass flow rate, but a very high exhaust velocity (600 m/s and more). The dominant noise source was clearly the exhaust system and the mixing of the jet with the ambient air.

The low bypass-ratio turbofan engine of the sixties, with a bypass-ratio of about 1.5, featured a higher air mass flow intake rate, but a lower exhaust velocity of the propelling jet. This made possible somewhat lower jet noise, but at the same time the turbomachinery noise increased. Typical transport aircraft using such engines were the B-727, B-707, DC-9, DC-8.

High bypass-ratio engines (with bypass-ratios of up to eight) process most of the intake air stream by the fan, with only a small portion passing to the core engine. Exhaust velocities of 300 m/s of the fan flow, and 400 m/s of the core engine flow are low enough to place jet noise second to fan turbomachinery noise, which is now the dominant noise source.

Gas turbine engine noise can be divided into two general categories: *internally* generated noise, usually associated with the rotating machinery, and *externally* generated noise, or jet noise.

Primary sources for internally generated noise are fan, compressor, and turbine (**Fig 10-2**). In most high bypass-ratio engines, the fan is the dominating noise source. Fan noise propagates out of the inlet and

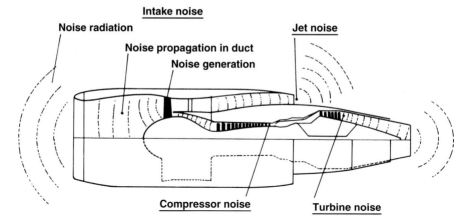

Fig 10-2   Internal noise sources

the fan discharge duct. Compressor noise also propagates out of the inlet, whereas turbine noise exits through the exhaust nozzle of the core engine.

Noise estimation
According to Lighthill's theory, the radiated sound intensity may be written as:

$$P \approx \rho d^2 c^n$$

with ρ air density, d nozzle exit diameter, c exhaust velocity.

Noise level, therefore, will increase with engine mass flow rate (being proportional to air density ρ) and the square of the diameter d of the noise source. The influence of velocity c can only roughly be estimated, by assuming a value for the exponent n.

Jet noise reduction
At high exhaust velocities of the jet (about 400 to 500 m/s), radiated sound intensity rises as the eighth power of the exit velocity (n = 8), whereas at low exhaust velocities (about 200 m/s) radiated sound intensity rises only as the second power (n = 2). A reduction in jet noise can therefore be expected from engines having high bypass-ratios with attendant low exhaust velocities. Investigations had shown long before the advent of the high bypass-ratio engine, that at a bypass-ratio of 10, noise could be reduced by 50 per cent (– 10 PNdB).

Before high bypass-ratio engines became available for civil aviation, inventive technical solutions for the suppression of noise had to be found. One of these solutions was the lobe-type nozzle of the early sixties, which split the exhaust jet into many smaller jets (**Fig 10-3**).

Fig 10-3   Method of splitting up the exhausting jet as was common with low bypass-ratio engines of the seventies

Noise suppression results from the mutual shielding of individual jets, together with a better mixing of the jets with the ambient air. Mixing was enhanced by the greatly enlarged contact surfaces that promoted rapid decay in jet velocity. A lobe-type nozzle was used on the Boeing 707, for example.

The same effect can be achieved with a nozzle featuring external corrugations that allow atmospheric air to flow into the exhausting jet to promote rapid mixing. The mixing process reduces jet velocity and, hence, noise.

Noise reductions from such nozzles were sizable, but by present-day noise standards, certification could never be granted. Moreover, thrust losses amounted to 1 per cent per 1 PNdB noise suppression.

Fan noise
As bypass-ratio was increasing over the years, manufacturers were faced with increasing levels of fan noise – a problem which proved more laborious than jet noise. Fan noise is internal noise associated with turbomachinery. As fan blades rotate, eddies emanate from blade trailing edges causing a broad noise spectrum. Additionally, due to flow displacement from blades, a discrete tone is generated which depends on blade tip speed. A further noise source is the boundary layer wake of a preceding blade impinging on a following blade and impairing that blade's aerodynamic characteristics. Such effects, however, diminish with increased blade spacing.

The acoustic characteristics of the fan are basically determined by three parameters of its aerodynamic design:

  – the spacing between rotor and stator

- the number of rotor and stator blades
- the rotor blade tip speed

By increasing the spacing between rotor and stator blades, a noise reduction of 6 to 8 PNdB can be achieved. The disadvantage, however, is the greater length of the engine and the higher weight incurred. The relatively large spacing necessary for noise reduction usually degrades fan efficiency by 1 per cent.

The number of blades is also a factor that affects noise characteristics. Good fan efficiency calls for a relatively large number of blades which happens also to be beneficial for noise characteristics, because aerodynamic loading can be spread over more blades, and noise rises with aerodynamic loading. More blades could also mean less weight for the fan assembly (fan disk, casing, blades) and a reduced structural length of the component.

On the other hand, when opting for a reduced number of blades, compressor surge characteristics will improve if fan blade tip speed is unchanged. Also, manufacturing costs may be less. The number of blades finally selected will be a compromise of diverse factors.

The typical relation between numbers of fan stator blades and fan rotor blades in high bypass-ratio engines is about 2. Increasing the

Fig 10-4   Noise suppressors used on a Boeing 707 during the seventies

Fig 10-5   Noise suppressor on Rolls-Royce Spey low bypass-ratio engine used in the seventies

number of stator blades could reduce fan noise by 5 PNdB. The tendency of blades to vibrate will, however, increase, whilst the fan surge margin will shrink at the same time.

Choice of fan tip speed will also affect fan noise. The lowest noise level will be achieved if tip speed is subsonic, but then the required stage pressure ratio of 1.5 cannot be attained with a single-stage fan. The lowest economic tip speed is considered to be in the range of 300 m/s (1000 ft/s) which means that reducing noise by lowering the tip speed is not possible.

A powerful noise reduction potential exists, however, in the aero-dynamic design of the air intake. The most notable option is a well-rounded intake lip which allowed the elimination of blow-in doors on early high bypass-ratio engines. Blow-in doors open automatically at high thrust settings to provide additional airflow to the fan, but intense noise can escape directly through doors. Despite the weight and length of intakes with rounded lips, this is the only type of intake found in modern engines.

Another method of reducing intake noise is by using sound-absorbing material for the intake duct. Such material incorporates a multitude of small resonant cavities which damp out acoustic pressure

Fig 10-6   Early high bypass-ratio turbofans featured auxiliary intake doors through which turbomachinery noise could escape. Outboard engine is of new design without doors, now common to all intakes of subsonic transport aircraft (test flight Boeing 747)

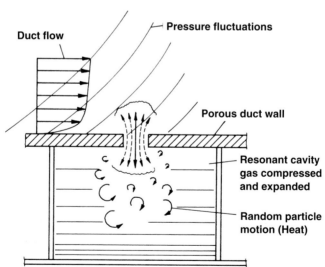

Fig 10-7   Functioning of porous wall to attenuate noise

fluctuations by allowing fluctuant air to enter and exit through a porous wall (**Fig 10-7**). By this method acoustic energy is converted into a disorderly particle motion and eventually into heat.

The quest for intake noise reduction produced a number of

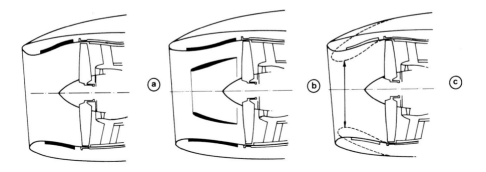

Fig 10-8 Methods of reducing fan turbomachinery noise
a) sound absorbing wall at intake duct (present method used
in practice)
b) concept of long intake duct with concentric splitter
c) variable geometry intake concept featuring sonic barrier

intelligent solutions which, however, did not materialize. One of those
designs proposed a concentric splitter installed in the intake duct,
which was to be equipped on both sides with sound-absorbing
material; another proposed a variable-geometry intake designed to
establish sonic velocity at the throat. Noise cannot escape through such
a sound barrier. At present, for reasons of simplicity, cost and weight,
the fixed-geometry intake is used exclusively, with sound absorbing
material employed along the duct walls.

10.2 Exhaust emissions

Gas turbine engines use hydrocarbons as fuel and the oxygen of the
ambient atmosphere as an oxidant. Due both to incomplete combustion and the heat of the combustion process, the jet exhausting from
the nozzle contains pollutants which are considered hazardous to life
on earth. Such pollutants are:

– carbon monoxide (CO)

- unburned hydrocarbons (CH_n)
- unburned carbon (C)
- nitric oxides (NO_x)

The typical combustion process
Pollutants are generated during the combustion process by a chemical
reaction which, due to the complicated interrelation of fluid dynamic
and combustion phenomena, is still insufficiently accessible by analyt-
ical methods. Descriptive methods are, therefore, largely of a
qualitative nature.

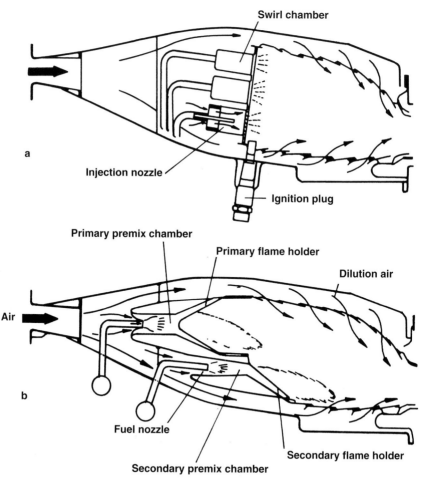

Fig 10-9   Combustion chamber concepts to reduce pollutants
a) swirl can combustor featuring staged fuel supply
b) staged premix combustor featuring staged combustion

In a typical combustor, airflow from the compressor enters the combustor through a diffusing section. Approximately one-fourth of the airflow enters the combustor primary zone either through swirlers or holes. Fuel is also injected in the primary zone where it mixes with air. In the primary zone, combustion is initiated, leading to a steep rise of temperature. The remaining three-quarters of the airflow bypasses the primary zone and enters the secondary and tertiary zones of the combustion chamber (Chapter 5). In the secondary zone, combustion is completed, while in the tertiary zone mixing with diluting air causes a drop in temperature. Zones in a combustion chamber are not physically separated from one another, making the chemical reaction a continuing process that extends over the whole combustor length.

Flow in the combustor changes greatly in individual zones, however. In the primary zone, flow is dominated largely by recirculation which is vital for combustion. In subsequent zones, flow is gradually aligned in the axial direction, and temperature homogenized by the incursion of dilution air.

Turbulent fluctuations in the primary zone result in large variations of gas resident times which, together with high temperatures, cause rapid changes in the concentrations of combustion products. This process determines the composition of the exhaust gas.

Another factor affecting exhaust gas composition is the development of the temperature in the combustor. In the primary zone, temperature rises steeply to a maximum value of 2,200K, but at the combustion chamber discharge it has dropped to a 'cool' 1,200K.

Investigations have shown, for example, that a longer resident time of the gas in the rear section of the combustor greatly enhances the conversion of carbon to carbon-monoxide – a method that eliminated the smoke trail of early engines. Also, if the maximum temperature in the primary zone can be kept at a low 1,800K, formation of nitric oxides will be impeded. This can be achieved by apportioning the primary air supply in accordance with engine thrust settings.

It can be seen that diverse environmental requirements must be satisfied in order to arrive at an optimized combustor, without undue compromise of engine performance. As environmental sensitivity grew, great efforts were made to comply with regulations, in particular those of the Environmental Protection Agency in the US. In its Experimental Clean Combustor Program of the seventies, NASA made great progress in combustor technology, as manifested by the following examples:

- in an experimental combustion chamber for the JT9D engine (that powers the B-747), individual combustors were replaced by three swirl-can combustors which greatly reduced nitric oxide content of the gas.

– an even temperature profile was obtained with another experimental combustion chamber featuring staged combustion and a premixing zone for fuel and air.

The results from such investigations have found widespread applications in modern engines.

11 Engine/airframe integration

One of the major tasks in the development of new aircraft is to ensure optimum compatibility between engine and airframe. This requires a thorough understanding of the complex fluid dynamic phenomena, which are usually studied during initial wind tunnel and theoretical investigations. The findings from such studies are necessarily applied to the real aircraft long before first flight. The task of properly integrating engine and airframe is of paramount importance to the success of a modern high-performance aircraft.

Integration aspects vary with the type of aircraft. In a subsonic civil transport, the fields addressed will be different from those for a supersonic combat aircraft.

11.1 Subsonic transport aircraft

The task of such aircraft is to transport people and freight. Engines are mounted on the wing or fuselage via pylons. Early attempts to bury engines in wing roots, as exemplified by the British Comet of the fifties, did not survive.

Three types of engine arrangements are currently used:

– underwing

– rear-fuselage

– mixed underwing/rear fuselage

Overwing arrangements were also attempted but are not pursued any more.

11.1.1 Underwing installation
The most frequently used disposition of engines is the underwing installation. This arrangement appears logical, because engine weight is carried where lift is generated. Wing bending moments are relatively small, which is beneficial to wing weight.

With respect to the airflow, however, the underwing installation is less beneficial. Due to the close vicinity of engine to wing, unfavourable flowfield interactions will occur. Large diameter high bypass-ratio turbofans, in particular, are very sensitive to interference effects. Great efforts are required to capitalize on the low specific fuel consumption

Fig 11-1   Underwing engine arrangement (Airbus A340)

of these engines in view of the interference drag resulting from improper installation.

Factors that adversely affect drag are (**Fig 11-2**):

- fan jet scrubbing,

- spillage of excess air,

- local supersonic velocity,

- friction.

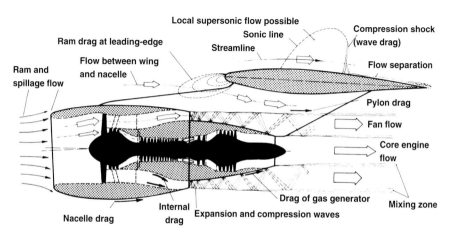

Fig 11-2   Flowfield characteristics of underwing installation

Fig 11-3   With engines mounted directly under the wing, flap cut-outs are necessary (Boeing 737-2000)

One factor directly entering into the drag bill is the fan jet scrubbing along fan cowl and pylon. The result is a loss of thrust.

A large-size fan cowl contributes considerably to aircraft drag, the amount being influenced by thrust setting. If the airflow requirement of the compressor is reduced, for example, so that the intake delivers more air than required, excess airflow will be spilled over. If spillage air separates from the intake lip, *spillage drag* will result.

Supersonic flow with attendant shock waves may occur at the rear of the fan cowl which results in *wave drag* as shock waves appear.

As the fan jet scrubs along the gas generator afterbody, *skin friction drag* in addition to wave drag, will result.

The fan discharge pressure ratio, together with gas generator geometry, will also give rise to loss of thrust. The discharge pressure ratio of modern high bypass-ratio engines is about 2.5 (i.e. total pressure at fan discharge to static ambient pressure). As this pressure ratio is super-critical, the fan jet will accelerate to supersonic velocity along the gas generator afterbody. Convex geometry of the afterbody aggravates this situation which will lead to drag-producing shock waves.

In general, the drag of a single nacelle may amount to 9 per cent of aircraft total drag. Components of nacelle drag are fan cowl drag 3.2%, drag of fan internal airflow 2.2%, gas generator drag 2.1% and pylon drag 1.5%.

What is still missing in our drag book-keeping is the drag resulting from the underwing installation of the engine. The nacelle and the underside of the wing together form a duct which is open on both sides. Excess velocities in the duct cause low pressure on the wing underside resulting in a downward aerodynamic force which opposes lift. To minimize such effects, engines are positioned away from the wing as much as possible. In practice, engine centreline position is arranged to be one nacelle diameter below the wing leading-edge, with the intake lip to be three-quarters of one nacelle length upstream of the wing leading-edge.

Early underwing installations, especially that of the Boeing 737-200, featured a direct engine/wing attachment, without a duct. The major advantage was shorter main undercarriage legs. This weight saving aspect had to be traded against a higher aerodynamic drag and a more complicated flap design requiring cut-outs around the engine.

Just as important in a wing installation is the selection of engine spanwise location. The benefits of placing the engine away from the fuselage to save wing weight are limited by one-engine-out controllability considerations. Certification requires that, in the case of asymmetric thrust caused by failure of one engine, the rudder must be capable of controlling the ensuing yawing moment. If engines are placed farther out, rudder size must be increased, which adds to airframe weight and aerodynamic drag.

In summary, many aspects have to be considered when placing engines under the wing. The optimum solution is mainly found from wind tunnel tests.

11.1.2 Fuselage installation

The reasons for installing engines at the rear fuselage instead of under the wing are primarily aerodynamic, as wing flow can be undisturbed from adverse engine effects. A fuselage installation is also beneficial when the aircraft is in the high lift configuration (flaps out for take-off and landing), because flaps can be installed along the full span between wing root and ailerons.

Aircraft which have all engines mounted on the rear fuselage, feature a T-shaped tail arrangement, with the horizontal tailplane mounted on top of the vertical stabilizer, or fin. One of the reasons for this is to prevent hot exhaust gas from adversely interfering with the tailplane.

However, a T-tail is not without problems when the aircraft is at high angles of attack. If the maximum permissible incidence is inadvertently exceeded, separated flow from the wing may cause the tailplane to stall which can render the aircraft uncontrollable. Also, engines may lose thrust because of improper flow to the intake rendering the aircraft unable to recover. A number of accidents, with many casualties, have been caused by this phenomenon. The best precaution is to bar certain angles-of-attack from attainment below prescribed minimum flight speeds.

Some earlier aircraft, notably the Lockheed TriStar and the Boeing 727, featured rear fuselage installations with the centre engine completely buried in the fuselage. Airflow to this engine was supplied through an S-shaped duct, with the air intake at the foot of the fin.

Fig 11-5   T-tail design required by aft-mounted engines (Boeing 727)

Fig 11-4   Aircraft powered by three large high bypass-ratio engines feature a mixed underwing/rear fuselage installation (McDonnell Douglas DC-10-30)

Because the thrust line of this engine coincides with the engine centre-line, engine failure causes no extra moment that needs to be balanced. Additionally, the rudder can be installed along the whole length of the fin trailing edge.

A disadvantage of the fuselage engine installation, however, is the large distance of the heavy engines from the aircraft's centre-of-gravity. This may give rise to problems when balancing the aircraft because the centre-of-gravity is sensitive to payload variations. In order to cope with this difficulty, it may even become necessary to carry sandbags in the forward fuselage when the payload is too low (as was the case with a certain Soviet airliner).

If engines grow beyond a certain size, the unfavourable effects of being too large and too heavy preclude an all-fuselage engine installation. In this case a mixed (underwing/rear fuselage) installation is a good solution, as pioneered by McDonnell Douglas with their DC-10 and MD-11 wide-body transports.

In general the rear-fuselage installation is a sound engineering solution to mounting engines on the airframe, which continues to be pursued with some modern airliners.

11.1.3 Overwing installation

One of the many attempts to combat aircraft noise gave new impetus to the overwing engine installation which was successfully pioneered with the VFW-Fokker 614 medium-range transport of the sixties. The basic idea was to eliminate the disadvantages both of the centre-of-gravity problem of the fuselage installation and the long landing gear legs of the underwing installation. Moreover, the high engine position could prevent damage from the ingestion of foreign objects – ideal assets for a civil (and military) transport aircraft when operating from remote or unprepared airstrips. Noise characteristics were also considered to be superior to other aircraft due to the wing's shielding high-frequency fan noise. The overwing installation was also considered in a Boeing project of that time.

Although this engineering solution appeared revolutionary, it did not survive. Having the engines on the sensitive upper (suction) surface of the wing, where excess velocities exist, makes the flow even more susceptible to disturbances from the pylon and the exhausting jet. As the jet also accelerates the upper-surface flow, local supersonic flow may occur, with consequent shock waves and attendant wave drag.

11.2   Combat aircraft

The operational requirements of combat aircraft call for small size, light weight and high manoeuvrability. A special characteristic is a high thrust-to-weight ratio which presently peaks at 1.4. A prerequisite in the design of high-performance combat aircraft is an advanced airframe together with high-thrust engines of low specific fuel consumption.

Fig 11-6   First airliner with overwing installation (VFW-Fokker 614 conceived in the sixties)

In contrast to subsonic aircraft, combat aircraft must operate over a large speed and altitude envelope, and must possess superior manoeuvrability. This requires a highly-efficient aerodynamic design of the airframe, which includes the interior surfaces of the engine duct. The task of integrating engine and airframe is hence intrinsically more demanding.

The interior engine installation determines the fuselage dimension and, in most cases, the position of wing and tailplane. Problems

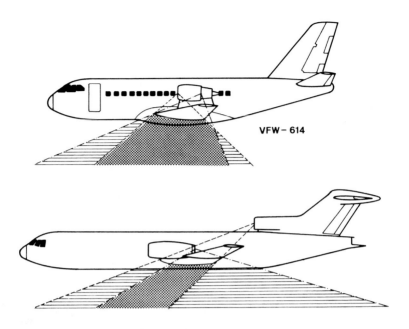

Fig 11-7   Noise shielding effect by overwing engine installation (top: VFW-Fokker 614, bottom: Boeing project 7X7, both of the sixties)

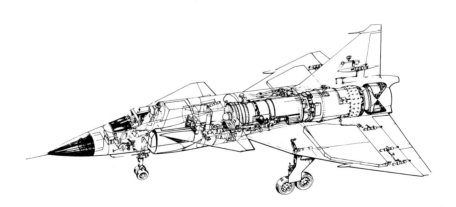

Fig 11-8   Efficient aerodynamic design of the airframe is supported by burying engines in the fuselage (SAAB Viggen)

resulting from the interior engine installation pertain to the intake and the aftbody of combat aircraft.

11.2.1 Intake installation considerations

The operational speed envelope of combat aircraft extends from subsonic to supersonic velocities, with maximum speed equivalent to Mach 2.5. Special high-speed aircraft such as the SR-71 and MiG-31, attain velocities at altitude of Mach 3+. Dog fights, which require high manoeuvrability, are usually flown at transonic speeds (around Mach 1). Fuel consumption is lowest during time-consuming subsonic cruising flight (combat air patrol sorties).

Maintaining aircraft performance over the entire speed envelope requires efficient design of the air intake (Chapter 3). Not only must the engine be supplied with a continuous high-quality airflow, the unfavourable effects of that flow on the airframe must also be minimized.

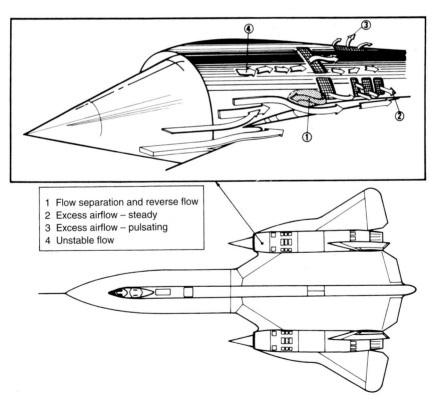

1 Flow separation and reverse flow
2 Excess airflow – steady
3 Excess airflow – pulsating
4 Unstable flow

Fig 11-9   Disturbed nacelle flowfield from dumping excess air (Lockheed SR-71)

Fig 11-10 Side-mounted air intakes
top: normal shock diffuser of SAAB Viggen
bottom: oblique shock diffuser of McDonnell Douglas F-4

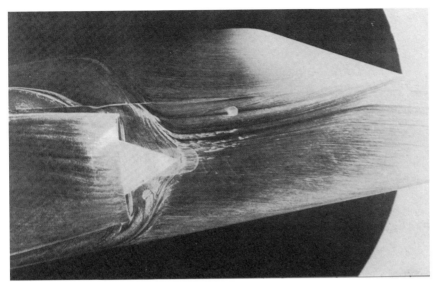

Fig 11-11 By using oil paint in wind tunnel, intake flow may be made visible (axisymmetric-type inlet, max airflow, 9 degrees incidence)

Intake characteristics are denoted by parameters such as total pressure recovery, distortion and turbulence. These refer to the compressor entry, and so pertain to the internal flow. Additionally, fluid dynamic effects on aircraft lift and drag (i.e. on the external flow) must also be considered.

Most of the intake losses result from excess air furnished by the intake. If engine airflow demand is less, excess air must be released to the ambient air. For example, if an air intake is designed for high supersonic velocities, then at transonic speeds excess airflow is provided which must be dumped overboard. This is done through special exhaust openings in the nacelle which inevitably causes drag by disturbing the external flowfield (**Fig 11-9**).

The choice of intake type depends on the primary mission for which the aircraft is designed. Combat aircraft operating within a large speed/altitude envelope will feature external compression intakes mounted to the sides of the fuselage. Such intakes operate as oblique-shock or as normal shock diffusers. The flowfield is influenced by a number of geometric factors such as fuselage forebody design including nose droop (F-4), canopy design, and intake position relative to the canopy.

Aerodynamic effects are usually investigated in the wind tunnel. While the bulk of testing comprises force and moment measurements, visualization of the flow is frequently made by using the oil painting technique.

In special cases where the combat mission requires long-endurance flying at high-supersonic Mach numbers (Mach 3+), without a need to manoeuvre, mixed-compression inlets are used which very efficiently diffuse the supersonic flow through a number of reflected shocks down to subsonic velocity. For such missions, external-compression inlets are not employed, because of their great aerodynamic drag at high supersonic Mach numbers.

11.2.2 Aftbody flowfield
The efficient integration of the exhaust nozzle with the aftbody became mandatory with the advent of multi-mission fighters. The task of aftbody integration is made more demanding because nozzle adaptation to varying Mach numbers and flight altitudes requires variable-geometry technology to be applied. Unfavourable mutual

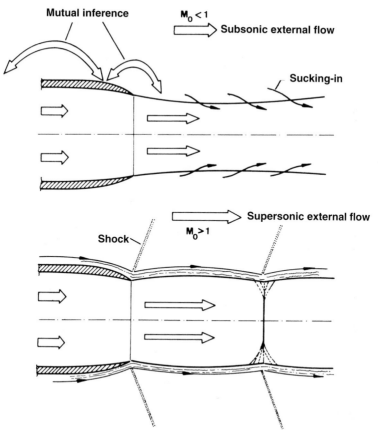

Fig 11-12 Interference effects between exhausting jet and aircraft rear fuselage at subsonic and supersonic flight speed (schematic)

Fig 11-13   The interfairing between engines greatly influences aftbody drag (top: McDonnell Douglas F-4 with low-drag vertical interfairing; bottom: Grumman F-14 with low-drag horizontal interfairing)

interference effects between the exhausting jet and the ambient atmosphere will adversely influence the pressure distribution on the aftbody, thereby causing the flow to separate. Flow separations may also occur in the nozzle, leading to a reduction of thrust. Efficient integration will keep losses of this kind to a minimum.

Fig 11-14   Complex interference effects occur with engines closely spaced (General Dynamics F-111)

A jet exhausting from the nozzle may be characterized by two important factors:

1 The jet behaves like a solid body that causes the external flow to be displaced.
2 The jet entrains air from the external flow causing the jet to expand laterally.

If the aircraft flies at *subsonic* velocities, typical jet-related effects may occur. The jet contour will act in an upstream direction to influence the flow on the aftbody which, if not properly integrated, will trigger flow separation on upstream areas of the fuselage (**Fig 11-12**, top).

If the aircraft flies at *supersonic* velocities, the spreading of upstream disturbances will be confined to subsonic portions of the boundary layer (**Fig 11-12**, bottom). However, shock waves emanating from the jet may impair tailplane effectiveness. Such effects have to be considered in the design of combat aircraft.

Combat aircraft feature either single or twin engine layouts, with interference effects that are particularly complex if the aircraft has side-by-side engine arrangements. The critical parameters for integration are engine lateral spacing, aftbody contouring and empennage arrangement.

Fig 11-15   Configurations with only a single vertical fin have less drag

At subsonic flight speeds, engine lateral spacing has only a minor effect on aircraft drag. At supersonic velocities, however, aircraft drag increases dramatically with spacing. For this reason, engines should be arranged as close as possible to one another. The interfairing between both nozzles, although of small size, has great influence on aircraft drag. If it is arranged as a vertical wedge, drag will be high because a low-pressure zone is built up between interfairing and conical aftbody, the resultant aerodynamic force of which opposes thrust. This adverse effect may be relaxed by extending the vertical-wedge interfairing in a downstream direction beyond the nozzle exit (F-4). Alternatively, a horizontally arranged interfairing will cause less drag.

Aircraft with a single fin inherently have less drag (**Fig 11-15**). Twin fins engender more drag, not only from greater surface area, but from interference drag although this can be minimized by canting the fins outwards as, for example, on the F-15.

Appendix 1 Commercial turbofan engines

Commercial turbofan engines

Manufacturer	Engine designation	Aircraft powered by engine	Components				Performance			Dimensions & weight		
			Compressor			Turbine	Take-off thrust	Specific fuel consumption	Mass flow rate (kg/s)	Fan diameter (m)	max length (m)	Dry mass kg (less nozzle)
			Number of stages (fan/lp + hp)	Pressure ratio	Bypass ratio	Number of stages (hp + lp)						
General Electric	CF6-80A	A310, B-767	1/3 + 14	27.7	4.28	2 + 4	220 kN (48,000 lb)	0.352	670	2.19	4.00	3,820
	CF6-80C2	B-747-300/400, B-767, A310 A300-600, MD-11	1/4 + 14	31	5.13	2 + 5	233-273 kN (52,500 + lb)	0.32-0.33	800	2.36	4.09	4,144
	CF6-80E1	A330	1/4 + 14	32	5.2	2 + 5	300-320 kN (67,500 + lb)	0.32-0.33	861	2.44	4.17	4,173
	GE90-85B	B-777	1/3 + 10		10	2 + 6	377 kN (84,700 lb)			3.35	4.88	
CFM International (General Electric + Snecma)	CFM56-5A3	A320-200, A319	1/3 + 9	28	5.96	1 + 4	118 kN static 22.3 kN @ cruise (26,500 lb st)	0.611 (cruise)	391	1.735	2.42	2,265
	CFM56-5B2	A321	1/4 + 9	33.6	5.43	1 + 4	137 kN static 26.2 kN @ cruise (31,000 lb st)	0.611 (cruise)	433	1.735	2.60	2,381
	CFM56-5C4	A340-200	1/4 + 9	34	6.36	1 + 5	151 kN static 31.5 kN @ cruise (34,000 lb st)	0.586 (cruise)	483	1.836	2.62	2,540
IAE (P&W, RR, MTU, Fiat, Jaec)	V2500-A1	A320-200	1/3 + 10	30	5.44	2 + 5	110 kN static 22.5 kN @ cruise (24,800 lb st)	0.598 (cruise)	360	1.6	3.20	2,367
	V2500-A5	A319, A320, A321	1/4 + 10	32.5	4.60	2 + 5	133 kN static 25.6 kN @ cruise (30,000 lb st)	0.606 (cruise)	384	1.6	3.20	2,240
	V2500-D5	MD-90-30, MD-90-50	1/4 + 10			2 + 5	146.8 kN static 28 kN @ cruise (33,000 lb st)			1.6	3.20	

Commercial turbofan engines

Manufacturer	Engine designation	Aircraft powered by engine	Compressor			Turbine	Take-off thrust	Specific fuel consumption kg/daN/h	Mass flow rate (kg/s)	Fan diameter (m)	Engine length (m)	Dry mass -less nozzle- (kg)
			Number of stages (fan/lp + hp)	Pressure ratio	Bypass ratio	Number of stages (hp + lp)						
	JT8D-200	MD-80 series aircraft	1/6 + 7	18		1 + 3	77-97 kN (...- 21,700 lb)	0.51-0.66		1.17	3.92	
	JT9D-7R4-E1	A310-300, B-767	1/4 + 11	23	5.0	2 + 4	222.4 kN takeoff 50.3 kN cruise (50,000 lb)	0.624 @ cruise	731	2.36	3.90	4,040
	PW4152	A310-300, A300-600,(B-747-400, B-767, MD-11 powered also by engines of PW4000 series)	1/4 + 11	27.3	5.0	2 + 4	231.3 kN takeoff 49.3 kN cruise (52,000 lb)	0.581 @ cruise	741	2.36	3.90	4,040
Pratt&Whitney	PW4168	A330-300	1/4 + 11	35.9	4.8	2 + 4	302.5kN takeoff 57.5 kN cruise (68,000 lb)	0.565 @ cruise	900	2.51	3.37	4,264
	PW4084	B777	1/6 + 11			2 + 7	376 kN takeoff (84,600 lb)					
	PW2136	A340-200	1/4 + 12	25.0	6.1	2 + 5	160 kN takeoff 35 kN cruise (36,000 lb)	0.565 @ cruise	532	2.03		
	PW2037	B757	1/4 + 12	30	5.8	2 + 5	170 kN takeoff (38,000 lb)	0.563 @ cruise	541	1.99	3.72	3,028
	RB211-524G /..H	B-747-400, B-767-300	1 + 7 + 6			1 + 1 + 3	258 kN - 270 kN	0.57		2.19	3.18	
Rolls-Royce	RB.211-535E4 /..E4B	B-757	1 + 6 + 6			1 + 1 + 3	178 -192 kN	0.598		1.88	2.99	
	Trent 768/772	A330	1 + 8 + 6			1 + 1 + 4	300-316 kN	0.565		2.47	3.90	

Appendix 2 Military turbofan engines

Military turbofan engines

Manufacturer	Engine designation	Aircraft powered by engine	Components Compressor — Number of stages (fan/lp + hp)	Pressure ratio	Bypass ratio	Turbine — Number of stages (lp + hp)	Take-off thrust	Specific fuel consumption	Mass flow rate (kg/s)	Fan diameter (m)	Engine length (m)	Dry mass kg (less nozzle)
Pratt & Whitney	F100-PW-220	F-16A/B, F-15	3 + 10	-	-	2 + 2	65 kN dry, 106 kN reheat			1.18	4.85	
	F100-PW-229	F-16, F-15	3 + 10	-		2 + 2	79 kN dry, 129 kN reheat			1.18	4.85	
	F117-PW-100	C-17 transport (engine is mil. version of civil PW2000 series)	1/4 + 12	-		2 + 5	185 kN	0.73		2.15	3.72	
	F119-PW-100	F-22 stealth fighter	3 + 6			1 + 1	157 kN reheat					
	F110-100	F-16C/D	3 + 9	30.4		1 + 2	78 kN dry, 125 kN			1.18	4.62	
	F110-400	F-14B/D re-engine	3 + 9	30.4		1 + 2	72 kN dry, 119 kN reheat			1.18	5.90	
General Electric	F118-100	B-2 (engine is non-afterburning F110 derivative)	3 + 9			1 + 2	85 kN no reheat			1.18	2.55	
	F404-402	F-18C/D	3 + 7	26.0		1 + 1	53 kN dry, 79 kN reheat	1.79		0.89	4.04	1,020
	F404-F1D2	F-117A (Stealth fighter)	3 + 7			1 + 1	47 kN no reheat			0.89	2.26	
	F404/RM12	Saab JAS39 Gripen	3 + 7	26.0		1 + 1	54 kN dry, 80.5 kN reheat	1.79		0.89	4.04	1,050
Rolls-Royce	Pegasus 11-61	Harrier II Plus	3 + 8			2 + 2	106 kN no reheat			1.22	3.48	
Snecma	M88-2	Rafale	3 + 6			1 + 1	50 kN dry, 75 kN reheat				3.54	
Turbo-Union (Rolls-Royce, MTU, FiatAvio)	RB.199-105	Tornado ECR	3/3 + 3 + 6			1 + 1 + 2	42.5 kN dry, 74.3 kN reheat			0.75	3.30	
Eurojet (MTU, FiatAvio, Rolls-Royce, ITP)	EJ200	Eurofighter 2000	1/3 + 5			1 + 1	60 kN dry, 90 kN reheat			0.74	4.00	

Index

splitter plates 76–9
spray nozzles 190–1
stable operating range 129
Starfighter, Lockheed F-104: 6,
    7, 68
Starlifter, Lockheed C-141: *11*,
    50–2
starters 201–3
starting 131 *see also* ignition
    systems 199–203
stator 136–7
    blades 94–5
    vanes, variable 111, 115–16
steam turbines 1, 2
streamlines 36–7
streamtubes 36–7
sump ventilation 197
supersonic configuration and
    operation 70–4
supersonic flows 56–69
    over wedge and cone 65–9, 72,
    80–2
surge, engine compressor 107,
    111–12

temperature 27, 111, 117, 127,
    146–7, 151–4
    distribution 129–31
tertiary inlet doors 162–5
thermal fatigue 152–3
thermodynamics, first law in 39
throttle lever positions 205
thrust *28*, 32–5, 40–1
    augmentation *see* afterburner
    bearing 123

measurement of 41–3
related to frontal area 41
reverser 167–74
specific 40–1, 43
specific fuel consumption
    (TSFC) 42
total pressure loss 128–9
turbine 136–54 *see also* gas
    turbine
    assembly – case studies 143–51
    blade cooling 146–8, 153
    blade design 142–3
    conical shafts 144
    constant-pressure 139–40
    design and operation 136–8
    disks 144–6
    nozzles 137, 138–9
    reaction 140
    rotor blades 140, 143
    stage 139–40
turbochargers 2
turbofan, definition of 3–4, 9–21
turbojet, definition of 3–6
turboprop, definition of 4, 6, 8
turboshaft, definition of 4, 21–2

underwing installation 219–22
units, system of 27, 41–2

VFW/Fokker 614: 56, 224, *225–6*
vibration 205
Viggen, Saab 170–4, *226*, *228*

water injection 182–3
Whittle, Sir Frank 2, 3